ReadyGEN

Text Collection

GRADE 6

PEARSON

Glenview, Illinois • Boston, Massachusetts • Chandler, Arizona • New York, New York

ISBN-13: 978-0-328-85287-1
ISBN-10: 0-328-85287-2
1 16

Table of Contents

Unit 3 Defining Courage and Freedom

Unit 4 Innovating for the Future

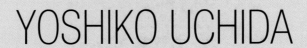

YOSHIKO UCHIDA

The
INVISIBLE THREAD

An excerpt from the memoir of the same name

My sister, Keiko (left), and I before World War II

Having a good time with our neighbors. Left to right, Solveig, Yoshiko, Marian, Keiko.

BECOMING A "NONALIEN"

"No company for lunch?" I asked, surprised.

It was Sunday, but there were only the four of us going home from church. It seemed strange, but I was glad for the peace and quiet. Finals were starting soon at the university, and I was anxious to have a quick lunch and go to the library to study.

As we were having lunch, an urgent voice suddenly broke into the program on the radio. Japan, the announcer said, had attacked Pearl Harbor.

"Oh, no!" Mama gasped. "It must be a mistake."

"Of course it is," Papa agreed.

He turned up the volume. It didn't sound like a mistake.

"It's probably the work of some fanatic," Papa insisted.

Not one of us believed it was war. Kay went with my parents to visit friends, and I went to the campus library to study. I didn't return until almost five o'clock.

The minute I got home, I knew something was wrong. A strange man sat in our living room, and my father was gone.

Mama and Kay explained that two FBI men had taken my father for questioning. A third remained to guard us, intercepting all phone calls and preventing friends from coming to see us.

"We're prisoners in our own home," Kay said ominously. "The police even broke in and searched our house while we were out."

As upset as she was, in her usual thoughtful way, Mama was making tea for the FBI man in the kitchen. She always served tea to anyone who called, even the "Real Silk Lady," who came with her satchel of silken samples to sell Mama stockings and undergarments.

"You're making tea for the FBI man?" I asked, indignant.

But Mama respected everybody regardless of the work they did. The man who delivered our dry cleaning, the People's Bread man who sold doughnuts and bread from his truck, the boy who delivered rice and tofu from the Japanese grocery store, or the Watkins door-to-door salesman. She treated them all with equal respect and courtesy.

"He's only doing his job," Mama said now of the FBI man. "He's trying to be pleasant." And she carried a tray of tea things into the living room.

But I wasn't about to have tea with someone guarding us as though we were prisoners. I went to my bedroom and stayed there until the FBI man got instructions to leave.

When at last the three of us were alone, we made supper, but none of us felt like eating. Papa was gone, and we had no idea what happened to him or when he would be back. We finally went to bed, leaving the porch light on for him.

As I lay in bed in my cold, dark room, I heard the mournful wail of the foghorns on the bay. I felt a clammy fear come over me, as though I was at the bottom of a deep well and couldn't climb out.

My father didn't return that night or for the next three days. We had no idea where he was or what had happened to him. But Mama persuaded me to continue going to classes, and somehow I managed to get through my finals.

Five days after he was taken, we finally learned that my father was being held at the Immigration Detention Quarters in San Francisco with about one hundred other Japanese men.

The FBI had apprehended all the leaders of the Japanese American community—businessmen, teachers, bankers, farmers, fishermen—and held them incommunicado.

The following day we got a postcard from Papa asking us to send his shaving kit and some clean clothing. We arranged for permission to visit him, and Kay drove us to San Francisco.

My heart sank when I saw the drab gray building that looked like a jail. And as though to confirm my impression, a guard brought Papa to the visiting room like a prisoner.

"Papa! Are you all right?"

He looked tired and haggard, but assured us that he was fine. The news he gave us, however, was terrible. All the men in his group were being sent in a few days to a prisoner-of-war camp in Missoula, Montana.

"Montana! Then we won't be able to visit you anymore."

"I know," Papa answered, "but we can write to each other. Now, girls, be strong, and take good care of Mama for me, will you?"

Kay and I began to cry as we said our good-byes and watched Papa go back down the bleak hallway. It was Mama who was the strong one.

From the moment we were at war with Japan, my parents (and all the Issei [Japanese-born immigrants]) had suddenly become "enemy aliens." They were not citizens because by law the United States prevented Asians from becoming naturalized citizens. Now Kay, as the oldest U.S. citizen, became head of our household.

She had graduated from Mills College in 1940 with a degree in early childhood education, but the only job she could find was as a nursemaid to a three-year-old white child. Her employers asked her to stay on in spite of the war, but I wondered why they felt compelled to say that. After all, Kay was still the same person, and she was an American, just as they were.

However, strange ideas seemed to be erupting in the minds of many Americans. I was astonished when a white friend of many years asked, "Didn't you have any idea it was going to happen?"

I was hurt that she had asked. Her question implied that we somehow knew of Japan's war plans simply because we were Americans of Japanese ancestry. It was a ridiculous assumption.

Eventually Kay left her job to devote all her time to managing our household affairs. Papa's bank account had been blocked immediately, and for a while we could withdraw only $100 a month for living expenses. She needed important papers from his safe-deposit box, but found that the FBI had confiscated all his keys.

She needed to pay the premiums on his car and life insurance policies, file his income tax returns, and at his request, purchase U.S. Defense Bonds. It was a difficult job for Kay, trying to manage all the tasks that Papa had handled until then.

Papa wrote often, trying to help us manage without him, but his letters often arrived looking like lace doilies. The censors had cut out whatever they didn't want us to read.

"Don't forget to lubricate the car," Papa wrote. Or, "Be sure to have the roses pruned, brush Laddie every day, send Grandma her monthly check, and take our Christmas offering to church."

We could tell he was trying to anticipate all our problems from his snowbound camp in Montana. He also tried to cheer us up, and asked us to tell our church friends not to be too discouraged.

Still, it was hard not to worry. Japan was now the despised enemy, and every Japanese American became a target of the same hatred directed at Japan. It was not because we had done anything wrong, but simply because we *looked* like the enemy.

Once again, my Japanese face was going to cause me misery.

One evening I went out with some friends for a late evening snack to a restaurant where we'd often gone before. We hadn't been there long when an angry Filipino man came to our table. His fists were clenched, and his eyes flashed with anger.

"You know what your Jap soldiers are doing to my homeland?" he shouted. "They're killing my people!"

"But we're not from Japan," we said, trying to reason with him. "We're Americans!"

He continued to harass us, not listening to anything we said. Then having had his say, he left, still scowling. But he had ruined our evening, for we knew there were many others who hated us as much as he did. We left the restaurant quickly and went home in silence.

I was frightened as I saw newspaper accounts accusing Japanese Americans of spying and sabotage in Hawaii.

These rumors were later completely refuted, but at the time most American's accepted them as the truth.

Soon racist groups began calling for a forced eviction of all Americans of Japanese ancestry along the West Coast. They called it an "evacuation"—a word implying removal for the protection of the person being removed—but actually it was an uprooting.

Hatred against Asians, however, was not new to California. It had existed for a hundred years. Laws that restricted immigration and land ownership already existed, and now groups who would benefit economically from our removal joined in the calls for a mass uprooting.

As new rumors spread, we grew more and more uneasy. Several of my classmates from out of town left the university to rejoin their families. And in Montana my father worried helplessly about what would happen to us.

We thought we should start packing some of our belongings, in case we were actually uprooted. One evening, as we were packing books into wooden crates, a friend stopped by to see us.

"What on earth are you doing?" he asked. "There will never be a mass evacuation. Don't you realize we're American citizens? The U.S. government would never intern its own citizens. It would be unconstitutional."

Of course his facts were right. Still, we knew that the attorney general of California claimed, incorrectly, that Japanese Americans had "infiltrated . . . every strategic spot" in the state.

On the floor of the House of Representatives, Congressman John Rankin had shouted, "I say it is of vital importance that we get rid of every Japanese . . . Let us get rid of them now!"

Our government did nothing to stop these hysterical outcries or to refute the false rumors. We learned many years later that although President Franklin D. Roosevelt had seen a state department report testifying to the "extraordinary degree of loyalty" among the West Coast Japanese Americans, he chose instead to listen to the voices of the hatemongers.

On February 19, 1942, the President signed Executive Order 9066, which resulted in the forcible eviction of all Japanese, "aliens and nonaliens," from the West Coast of the United States. He stated that this was a military necessity, and because we did not know otherwise at the time, we believed him. The Supreme Court of the land sanctioned his decision.

It was a sad day for all Americans of Japanese ancestry. Our government no longer considered us its citizens, simply referring to us as "nonaliens." It also chose to ignore the Fifth and Fourteenth Amendments to the Constitution that guaranteed "due process of law" and "equal protection under the law for all citizens." We were to be imprisoned in concentration camps without a trial or hearing of any kind.

"But we're at war with Germany and Italy, too," I objected. "Why are only the Japanese Americans being imprisoned?"

No one, including our government, had an answer for that.

Under the direction of Lieutenant General John L. DeWitt of the Western Defense Command, 120,000 men, women, and children of Japanese ancestry (two-thirds of whom were American citizens), were to be uprooted from their homes on the West Coast of the United States.

We were told we could "evacuate voluntarily" outside the military zone, but most of us had no place to go.

How could we suddenly pick up everything and move to a new and unknown location? Some of our friends moved to inland towns, but when the exclusion zone was later extended, they were uprooted once again and eventually interned in a camp anyway.

We felt like prisoners even before our actual eviction. We had to observe an 8:00 P.M. curfew and were not permitted to travel more than five miles beyond our home. We had to turn in all shortwave radios, cameras, binoculars, and firearms. We also had to register. Each family was given a number, and ours was 13453.

I shuddered when I read the headlines of our local paper on April 21. It read, "JAPS GIVEN EVACUATION ORDERS HERE." On May 1, we were to be sent to the Tanforan Racetrack, which had been hurriedly converted into an "Assembly Center."

"But how can we clear out our house in only ten days?" Mama asked desperately. "We've lived here for fifteen years!"

"I guess we just have to do it, Mama," Kay answered. "We can't argue with the U.S. Army."

Friends came to help us clear out our belongings. But no one could help us decide what to keep and what to discard. We had to do that for ourselves. We grew frantic as the days went by. We sold furniture we should have kept and stored things we should have thrown out.

Mama was such a saver. She had drawers and closets and cartons overflowing with memory-laden belongings. She saved everything from old string and wrapping paper to valentines, Christmas cards, clay paperweights, and drawings that Kay and I had made for her. She had dozens of photograph albums and guest books and packets of old letters from friends and family.

"How can I throw all this away?" she asked bleakly.

In the end she just put everything in trunks that we stored at the Bekins Storage Company. We also stored there the furniture that was too large to be left with friends offering us space in their basements.

We put off until the last minute a decision none of us wanted to make. What were we going to do with our beloved Laddie? We knew no friends who could take him. Finally, it occurred to me to put an ad in the *Daily Californian* at the university.

"I am one of the Japanese American students soon to be evacuated," I wrote, "and have a male Scotch collie that can't come with me. Can anyone give him a home? If interested, please call me immediately at Berkeley 7646W."

The day my ad appeared, I was deluged with sympathetic calls, but we gave him to the first boy who called because he seemed kind and caring. We gave him Laddie's doghouse, leash, brushes, favorite toy, and everything else he would need.

The boy promised he would write us at Tanforan to let us know how Laddie was doing. We each gave Laddie a hug and watched him climb reluctantly into the strange car.

"Be a good boy now, Laddie," I said. "We'll come back for you someday."

Mama, Kay, and I couldn't bear to go inside. We stood at the curb watching as the boy drove off. And we could still hear Laddie's plaintive barking even after the car turned the corner and we could no longer see it.

PRISONER OF MY COUNTRY

Papa's beautiful garden was now full of gaping holes. Mama had dug up a few favorite plants to give to her friends, and others were given to people like the woman who stopped by one day to ask if she could have some gladiolas. "Since you're leaving anyway . . ." she said, smiling awkwardly.

Our rented house was now a barren shell, with only three mattresses left on the floor. In the corner of Mama's room was a large shapeless canvas blanket bag that we called our Camp Bundle. We tossed into it all the things we were instructed to take with us—sheets, blankets, pillows, dishes, and eating utensils. We also added our own list of necessities—boots, umbrellas, flashlights, teacups, a hot plate, a kettle, and anything else we thought might be useful in camp.

"You know, we're supposed to bring only what we can carry," Kay warned.

We practiced lifting our suitcases and found that we could each carry two. But what were we to do about the Camp Bundle?

Each day it grew and bulged like some living thing, and we had no idea how we would ever get it to camp.

Still, there was nothing we could do but continue to fill it, and to hope that somehow things would work out.

The night before we left, our Swiss neighbors invited us to dinner. Mrs. Harpainter made a delicious chicken dinner, served on her finest china and linens, reminding me of all the company dinners we'd had in our own house in happier days.

When we got home, Marian and Solveig came from next door to say good-bye, bringing gifts for each of us.

They hugged us, saying, "Come back soon!"

"We will," we answered. But we had no idea when or if we would ever come back.

The next morning Mrs. Harpainter brought us breakfast on a tray full of bright colorful dishes. She then drove us to the First Congregational Church of Berkeley, designated as the Civil Control Station where we were to report.

We said our good-byes quickly, unable to speak many words. Already the church grounds teemed with hundreds of bewildered Japanese Americans, clutching bundles tagged with their names and family number. Parked at the curb were rows of trucks being loaded with the larger baggage that could not be hand-carried.

"I wish they had told us there'd be trucks," Kay muttered. "We could have been spared all that worry about our Camp Bundle."

But the army didn't seem to care whether we worried or not. To them we were simply prisoners. They had stationed armed guards all around the church, their bayonets mounted and ready. It was only when I saw them that the full horror of the day struck me. My knees felt weak, and I almost lost my breakfast.

The First Congregational Church had been good to us. Many of its families had offered to store belongings for the departing Japanese Americans, and now the church women were serving tea and sandwiches. But none of us could eat.

We were soon loaded onto waiting buses and began our one-way journey down familiar streets, across the Bay Bridge, and down the Bayshore Highway. Although some people wept quietly, most of us were silent. We kept our eyes on the window, watching as familiar landmarks slipped away behind us one by one.

And then we were there—at the Tanforan Racetrack Assembly Center, one of fifteen such centers created at racetracks and fairgrounds along the West Coast to intern the Japanese Americans.

From the bus window I could see a high barbed-wire fence that surrounded the entire area, and at each corner of the camp was a guard tower manned by soldiers.

The gates swung open to receive the buses, and armed guards closed them behind us. We were now locked in and under twenty-four-hour guard.

We had always been law-abiding citizens. We had done nothing wrong. And yet, we had now become prisoners of our own country.

———————————

There was an enormous crowd gathered around the grandstand. One would have thought the horses were running, except that all the people there were Japanese of all ages, sizes, and shapes.

We scanned the crowd for familiar faces and were relieved to find several friends who had arrived a few days earlier from Oakland.

"Hey, Kay and Yo! Over here!"

They steered us through the crowds to an area where doctors peered down our throats and pronounced us healthy. Then they helped us find our way to Barrack 16, Apartment 40, to which we had been assigned.

"We get apartments?" I asked.

"Not the kind you're thinking of, Yo. Wait, you'll see." My friend knew I was in for a rude awakening.

Mama was wearing her hat, gloves, and Sunday clothes, simply because she never would have thought of leaving home any other way. In her good Sunday shoes, she was carefully picking her way over the puddles left in the muddy track by rain the day before.

The army had hastily constructed dozens of tar-papered barracks around the track and in the infield to house the eight thousand "evacuees," as we were called. Each barrack was divided into six rooms, one family to a room. But our barrack was not one of these.

Barrack 16 turned out to be nothing more than an old stable, with twenty-five stalls facing north, back to back with the same number facing south. Our so-called apartment was a small, dark horse stall, ten feet by twenty feet. I couldn't believe what I saw.

Dust, dirt, and wood shavings littered the linoleum, and I could still smell the manure that lay beneath it. There were two tiny windows on either side of the door (our only source of daylight), and the stall was divided into two sections by a Dutch door worn with teeth marks.

On the walls I saw tiny corpses of spiders and bugs that had been permanently whitewashed to the boards by the army painters. A single light bulb dangled from the ceiling, and three folded army cots lay on the dirty floor. This was to be our "home" for the next five months.

One of our friends found a broom and swept out our stall, while two of the boys went to pick up our mattresses. Actually, they'd had to stuff the tickings with straw themselves.

Another friend loaned us some dishes and silverware since our big bundle hadn't yet been delivered. "We'd better leave soon for the mess hall before the lines for supper get too long," she warned.

Until smaller mess halls could be built throughout the camp, all meals were being served in the basement of the grandstand. Clutching our plates and silverware, we made our way back down the muddy track.

When we arrived at the grandstand, there were already several long weaving lines of people waiting to get in, and we were soon separated from our friends. Mama, Kay, and I took our places at the end of one line and huddled together to keep warm. A cold, piercing wind had begun to blow as the sun went down, and it scattered dust and debris in our faces.

I felt like a refugee standing in a soup line in some alien and forbidding land. It was not only degrading and humiliating, it seemed totally unreal—like some horrible nightmare.

Since we had missed lunch, I was eager for a nice hot meal, but supper consisted of a piece of butterless bread, two canned sausages, and a plain boiled potato. Everything was dropped onto our plates by two cooks, who picked up the food with their fingers from large dishpans.

We ate at picnic tables in the cold, damp basement crowded with hundreds of people, and even though I was still hungry, I couldn't wait to get back to our stall.

It was dark now, and the north wind was blowing into our stall from all the cracks around the windows and the door.

We bundled up in our coats and sat on our prickly mattresses, too miserable even to talk.

Kay and I worried that the cold air would aggravate Mama's neuralgia, which caused terrible pain in her facial nerves.

"Are you OK, Mom?" we asked.

But Mama wasn't thinking about herself. "I wonder how Papa San is?" she said softly.

Then we heard a truck outside, and a voice called, "Hey Uchida! Apartment 40!"

As Kay and I rushed to the door calling, "That's us!" we saw two baggage boys wrestling our big Camp Bundle off their truck.

"What ya got in here anyways?" they asked good-naturedly. "Didja bring everything . . .?"

I was embarrassed. Our bundle was clearly the biggest and bulkiest object in their truck.

"It's just our pet rhinoceros," I quipped. And while the boys were still laughing, we dragged our monstrous bundle into the stall and quickly untied all the knots we'd labored over just that morning.

Everything we had tossed into its obliging depths now tumbled out looking like old friends.

"I'll go get some water," I volunteered.

I grabbed the kettle and hurried to the women's latrine-washroom about fifty yards from our stable. Kay and Mama, in the meantime, retrieved our sheets and blankets to make up the cots.

I had news for them when I returned.

"There're no doors to the toilets or showers," I reported, horrified. "And we have to wash up at long tin sinks that look like feeding troughs."

I had also taken a look at the laundry barrack with its rows of washtubs, where everything, including sheets and towels, were to be washed by hand. They were still empty, but by morning there would be long lines of people waiting to use the tubs.

Mama diverted our attention to matters at hand. "Well, we can at least make some tea now," she said.

We plugged the hot plate into a double socket we'd had the good sense to bring and waited for the water to boil.

Then came the first of many knocks we'd be hearing at our door, as friends discovered where we lived.

"Hey, Kay and Yo. Are you home?"

Four of my college friends had come by to see how we were doing, bringing along the only snack they could find—a box of dried prunes. Even the day before, I wouldn't have given the prunes a second look. But now they were as welcome as a box of the Maskey's chocolates Papa used to bring home from San Francisco.

We gathered around the warmth of the hot plate, sipping the tea Mama made for us, wondering how we had gotten ourselves into such an intolerable situation.

We were angry that our country had so cruelly deprived us of our civil rights. But we had been raised to respect and trust those in authority. Resistance or confrontation such as we know them today was unthinkable, for the world then was a totally different place.

There had yet been no freedom marches or demonstrations of protest. No one had yet heard of Martin Luther King, Jr. No one knew about ethnic pride. Most Americans were not concerned about civil rights and would not have supported us had we tried to resist the uprooting.

We naively believed at the time that cooperating with the government was the only way to prove our loyalty and to help our country. We did not know then, as we do today, how badly our leaders betrayed us and our country's democratic ideals.

They had imprisoned us with full knowledge that their action was not only unconstitutional, but totally unnecessary. They knew there was no military necessity for the mass uprooting, although that was the reason given for incarcerating us.

How could America—our own country—have done this to us? we wondered. And trying to cheer ourselves up, we talked about steaks and hamburgers and hot dogs as we munched on the cold dried prunes.

Our family in happier days after WWII.

24

EPILOGUE

There is a footnote to add regarding the wartime uprooting. Some forty years after that tragic event, our country acknowledged at last that it had made a terrible mistake.

In 1976, President Gerald R. Ford stated, "Not only was that evacuation wrong, but Japanese Americans were and are loyal Americans."

In 1982, a commission established by President Jimmy Carter and the United States Congress concluded after an exhaustive inquiry that a grave injustice had been done to Japanese Americans, and that the causes of the uprooting were race prejudice, war hysteria, and a failure of political leadership.

In 1988, a Redress Bill was passed by Congress to mitigate some of the massive financial losses suffered by the Japanese Americans, but it was not put into effect until October 1990. It came too late for most of the Issei who, like my own parents, were gone, and too late for many Nisei [children of Japan-born immigrants] as well.

I have written several short stories and books that tell of this wartime uprooting, and each time I find it hard to believe that such a thing actually took place in the United States of America. But it did.

I find it painful to continue remembering and writing about it. But I must. Because I want each new generation of Americans to know what once happened in our democracy. I want them to love and cherish the freedom that can be snatched away so quickly, even by their own country.

Most of all, I ask them to be vigilant, so that such a tragedy will never happen to any group of people in America ever again.

Stories of
Courage

by Lydia Okutoro-Seck

When faced with a difficult challenge, many of us might not have the strength or nerve that it takes to persevere. The four notable individuals profiled here, however, have confronted personal adversity with remarkable courage and determination. Though their stories and experiences are very different, these brave people serve as a testament to the power and resilience of the human spirit.

Yoshiko Uchida
From War Prisoner to Celebrated Author

Imagine being forced to live with your family in a horse stall at a racetrack, where you reside for months until you are transferred to an even harsher desert camp. Your new "home" is surrounded by barbed wire. Armed guards monitor your every move. If you try to escape, then you risk being shot.

You are a prisoner of war, but you are not a soldier. You are actually a civilian. Your government has ordered your detainment because your country is at war, and people say you look like the enemy.

This is exactly what happened to Yoshiko Uchida. She was only twenty years old.

A Happy Childhood

Yoshiko was a U.S. citizen born in California on November 24, 1921, to Japanese immigrants. She was a *Nisei,* or a second-generation Japanese American. Yoshiko and her older sister, Keiko, enjoyed a happy home life. Their father, Takashi, had called himself "Dwight" since arriving in America. He worked as a manager at a major international trading company. Their mother, Iku, spent her days writing poetry while raising the girls.

In Berkeley, California, Yoshiko's family lived in a sun-filled, three-bedroom house. In the large backyard, peach and apricot trees grew. Like other American families, the Uchidas lived a comfortable life, with good schools and friendly neighbors.

Yoshiko did well in school. She was a diligent student and graduated early from high school. When she was sixteen years old, she was one of the youngest students to enroll at the University of California at Berkeley. Her future seemed full of endless possibilities.

Then, in December 1941, Japan bombed Pearl Harbor, launching the United States into World War II. Everything changed dramatically for Yoshiko and her family.

Stranger in a Desert Home

The bombing caused nationwide panic. People didn't know whom to trust or when the next attack might occur. This fear and distrust led to discrimination against Japanese Americans, as their fellow citizens suspected them of siding with the enemy.

On February 19, 1942, President Franklin Roosevelt issued Executive Order 9066. The law permitted the government to round up more than 120,000 Americans of Japanese ancestry. These innocent people were forced to leave their jobs, schools, and homes.

Law-abiding and loyal American citizens were detained and questioned. Many of them were immigrants who had left Japan for better lives in America. Others were born in the United States and knew it as their only home.

Yoshiko, Keiko, and their parents were ordered to leave their home, taking only what they could carry. First, the family lived in the Tanforan Assembly Center in California, which was actually a racetrack originally built for horse races. The U.S. government turned the racetrack into a temporary processing center where more than 5,000 California residents were processed during the war. At Tanforan, the Uchidas crammed into a horse stall and had to live there for months while waiting to be relocated.

Families were relocated under the watchful gaze of U.S. soldiers.

WESTERN DEFENSE COMMAND AND FOURTH ARMY
WARTIME CIVIL CONTROL ADMINISTRATION
Presidio of San Francisco, California
May 3, 1942

INSTRUCTIONS
TO ALL PERSONS OF
JAPANESE
ANCESTRY

Living in the Following Area:

A woman stands in the doorway of a converted horse stall at Tanforan.

Tule Lake, California (18,789)

Minidoka, Idaho (9,397)

Heart Mountain, Wyoming (10,767)

Amache/Granada, Colorado (7,318)

Manzanar, California (10,046)

Topaz, Utah (8,130)

Rohwer, Arkansas (8,475)

Poston, Arizona (17,814)

Gila River, Arizona (13,348)

Jerome, Arkansas (8,497)

People were detained at temporary processing centers like Tanforan while the U.S. government built relocation camps around the country to house thousands of Japanese Americans. The maximum population of each camp is shown on the map.

In 1942, after five months in Tanforan, Yoshiko and her family received their relocation assignment. They were moved to an internment camp called Topaz, where they were confined and held in custody. Topaz was one of ten internment camps across the United States during World War II. Located in the middle of the Utah desert, it was many miles from California—far from Yoshiko's home.

The Uchida family's living quarters in Topaz were slightly larger than the horse stall at Tanforan. Each barrack contained five or six rooms, and up to eight people shared each room. Tar paper covered and separated the rooms, offering little privacy for families. The barracks did not include kitchens or bathrooms, and there were no separate bedrooms. Yoshiko and her family had to share communal toilets and showers located in a separate part of the camp, and the lines for the toilets seemed endless. Similarly, hundreds of people waited for food in lines that snaked around the camp.

Yoshiko and the other detainees lived in exile, isolated from the rest of the country. Surrounding the barracks was desert and open space, and the climate was brutal. Summers were extremely hot and winters unbearably cold, while snakes and scorpions sometimes made their way into the rooms and shared the space with Yoshiko and her family. For Yoshiko, Topaz was a city of dust and despair.

The Topaz internment camp was located in the Utah desert.

Free to Tell Her Stories

During her internment at Topaz, Yoshiko faced her isolation with determination and courage. She took advantage of what opportunities were available. Filled with a love for literature passed on from her mother, Yoshiko wrote stories while interned at Topaz. Writing became a passion that helped her survive.

She taught second-grade classes at the camp, for which she was paid $16 a week. She maintained the same diligence she had before the internment. In 1942, Yoshiko received her degree from the University of California, but she was unable to attend her graduation ceremony. In 1943, Keiko and Yoshiko were allowed to leave the internment camp for Massachusetts, where Keiko had been offered a job at Mount Holyoke College and Yoshiko a fellowship at Smith College. Their parents left Topaz near the end of the war, when the government finally closed the camps.

As Yoshiko grew older, her written work earned her awards and accolades. Through her folktales and nonfiction stories, she was able to explore her Japanese ancestry and culture.

Yoshiko won a grant that allowed her to travel to Japan after the war. When she returned to America, she penned more stories that gave meaning to her wartime experience. She published dozens of books for children and adults, using her life stories to educate others about topics such as identity, cultural pride, and tolerance.

Yoshiko Uchida died in 1992 after contributing more than twenty books to American literature. Through her writing, she taught young people to never use labels to separate themselves from one another, and to face life's challenges with grace and hope.

Kyle Maynard

Reaching for the Top

Have you ever set a personal goal that seemed impossible to reach? Some people never try for many reasons. Some feel afraid, while others say they have no time. Some people think they lack the resources to succeed. But Kyle Maynard is not one of those people who makes excuses. He is as fearless as they come.

Kyle is a quadruple amputee. He has no arms below his elbows and no legs below his knees. Yet he is a title-winning wrestler and a decorated mixed martial arts fighter. He has climbed to the top of Mount Kilimanjaro, the tallest peak in Africa and the highest freestanding mountain in the world.

A Normal Boyhood

When Kyle was born on March 24, 1986, his parents, Scott and Anita, were shocked to learn that their infant boy suffered from congenital amputation, a condition that occurs in the womb. Some children born with the disorder are missing fingers or toes. Kyle's was a rare case that affected all four of his limbs.

Growing up in Washington, D.C., Kyle had the energy and curiosity of a typical boy. He wanted to try everything, and his parents encouraged him, driven by the desire for him to live a normal life. Of course, for several years after Kyle was born, his family did everything for him. However, one day his father announced that Kyle would have to learn to do things for himself. It was a big challenge, but Kyle never gave up, and he learned to become more independent as a result.

When Kyle was eleven, he joined a youth league football team and played the position of nose tackle. Kyle was about half the size of most other players. He didn't get the same amount of playing time as other members of the team. But Kyle never gave up on the hard work involved in training to be the best athlete. He doubled his efforts and focused on his strengths instead of on his disability.

The following year, Kyle joined his school's wrestling team. He lost his first match and all his other matches that year. But losing didn't deter Kyle. He trained harder and with more determination each year. Eventually, after losing dozens of matches, he began to succeed and won thirty-six matches in his senior year.

A Winner's Spirit

By the time he joined his high school wrestling team, Kyle had developed a spirit of unrelenting willpower and courage. These traits would help to take him further and higher than most people who have full use of their limbs. His personal philosophy is to make no excuses because there are no such things as barriers.

At the end of his high school career, Kyle Maynard was a state wrestling champion on his way to setting records for his athleticism. During his final wrestling season, he received an award for bench-pressing 240 pounds—more than double his weight!

In 2004, Kyle won a major award for athletes with disabilities, and a year later, he broke a world record by lifting 360 pounds. That same year, he published a best-selling book about his life story. With the support of his family and community, Kyle opened a fitness center in 2008. He also devotes much of his spare time to helping wounded military veterans. He has received the Highest Recognition Award of the Secretary of Health and Human Services for his humanitarian efforts.

Crawling Up Kilimanjaro

At age 25, Kyle set out on another seemingly impossible mission: to climb to the top of Mount Kilimanjaro. Located in Tanzania, East Africa, Kilimanjaro peaks at 19,341 feet. Many people have tried the ascent, but not all of them have succeeded. Kyle's goal was to crawl up the mountain on all fours like a bear—without the help of prosthetics. He also wanted to use the opportunity to raise awareness for wounded military veterans who had lost limbs in combat.

When he first announced his plans, people thought he was kidding. But as with his previous endeavors, Kyle was utterly serious. He prepared by training at mountains around the United States and, with help from friends, developed equipment to protect himself. Sharp, large rocks cover Kilimanjaro, so Kyle needed special equipment attached to his body with heavy-duty tape.

On January 6, 2012, Kyle and his team of 10 began the trek up Kilimanjaro. Everyone expected the journey to take 15 days.

During the ascent, Kyle showed his characteristic fearlessness. He crawled and dragged himself up the mountain with the group, hiking six to seven hours each day. Then Kyle seemed to reach a breaking point. The climb was getting treacherous. It all took a toll on Kyle physically and emotionally. His arms bruised and swelled up. He had to make a choice—either push beyond the mounting stress on his body or be airlifted off the mountain and end the mission.

But Kyle's will could not be broken. Before the trip to Africa, Kyle had promised the mother of a fallen soldier that he would carry her son's ashes to the top of Kilimanjaro. That promise helped Kyle forge ahead, and he gathered all his courage. The group's leader suggested a shorter but steeper route up the mountain. It was more dangerous. Six years earlier, three climbers were killed on that route. Kyle agreed to take the steeper route, saying, "I know I can do it. I mean, I know it for a fact." On January 15, 2012, Kyle became the first person in the world to crawl to the top of Mount Kilimanjaro, five days sooner than his goal.

Kyle Maynard is living proof that with strength and determination, there's no challenge that can't be conquered.

Kyle has traveled the world giving motivational speeches at corporate meetings, grade schools, and universities.

Malala Yousafzai

Defending Girls' Rights to Learn

A single, violent act propelled Malala Yousafzai into the public eye, allowing her to influence people all over the world. When gunmen attacked Malala, they thought they would silence the soft-voiced, outspoken schoolgirl. They were wrong. In response to their actions, a passionate movement for the rights of girls was launched in Pakistan and around the globe.

The Fearless Schoolgirl

Malala was born on July 12, 1997, in Mingora, Pakistan. Her father was a school principal who instilled the importance of education in his children, particularly in his only daughter. Her mother took care of their home and raised the children. Although her mother could not read or write, she was a quiet supporter of Malala and her two younger brothers. Malala thrived in school, often earning the top position in her classes.

Malala's hometown is located in the Swat Valley region of Pakistan. For Malala, it was a peaceful paradise with a beautiful landscape. The Taliban, a group of men from rural Pakistan and Afghanistan who practice an extreme interpretation of Islam, tried to destroy that paradise. The Taliban believe women and girls should be quiet and stay home. The men did not allow girls to attend school, go to the market, or dance.

In 2004, the Taliban arrived in Swat Valley and tried to enforce these restrictions, closing down schools or bombing them. They punished people for breaking their rules, and they executed those who openly opposed their way of life.

Malala and her father knew the risks, yet they courageously resisted the Taliban. Her father kept the school open for girls. Malala blogged about going to school under Taliban rule and spoke out about the injustices she witnessed. She must have been aware of the danger because she used a pseudonym to remain anonymous.

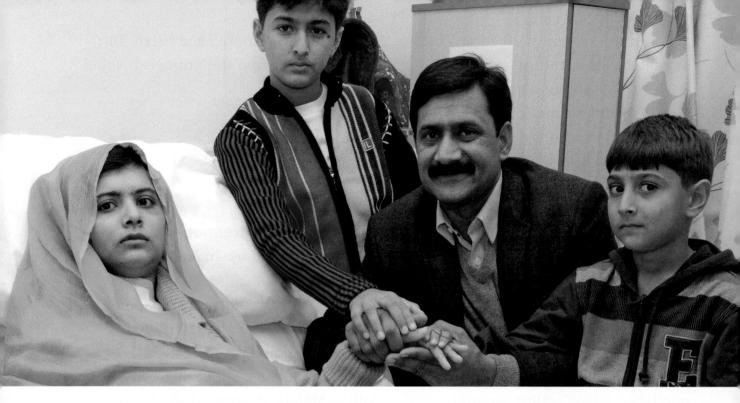

Over time, her commentaries and speeches reached a broad, international audience. She drew attention to the plight of Pakistani girls who were being injured or killed for wanting to attend school.

Influenced by her father's outspokenness against the Taliban, Malala agreed to reveal her blogging identity. She began making appearances on TV in Pakistan to speak about the issue of education. In December 2011, Pakistan bestowed on her the first National Youth Peace Prize. She hoped to use the newfound attention to start an education foundation.

Despite all the increased visibility, Malala was not afraid for herself. Instead, she feared for her father's life, especially because he already had received death threats.

An Attempt to Silence Her Voice

On the afternoon of October 9, 2012, Malala was on a school bus with other girls heading home after their exams. Two strangers approached the bus, demanding to know who among them was Malala. No one answered, but some of her friends looked at Malala. Three shots were fired, and one bullet hit Malala on the left side of her head and then lodged under her shoulder. The other bullets wounded two of her friends. Miraculously, fifteen-year-old Malala survived. She was taken to the hospital in another town for emergency surgery. Eventually, she was taken to specialists in Birmingham, England. There she could get the corrective surgery she needed.

The rest of her family left Swat Valley as well, never to return to Pakistan.

The assassination attempt on Malala made international headlines and caused immediate public outrage around the world. Although some people—including many in her own country—did not support Malala's message, most rallied around her and championed the cause for which she nearly died. The shooting gave her an even bigger platform to spread her message about every girl's right to an education, not just in Pakistan but also around the globe. In 2013, she published a best-selling memoir.

Malala is an inspiration to many and an undaunted public speaker and activist. She has addressed the United Nations, has earned numerous awards, and has been nominated twice for the Nobel Peace Prize. In 2014, she became the youngest Nobel Prize laureate.

Malala the Conqueror

All of the global attention unleashed a newfound courage in Malala. In one interview, she asserted that she was not afraid of terrorists. She said that they had already done the worst they could do and failed. It is as if the Taliban's bullet, instead of killing Malala, destroyed whatever fear she might have had before the shooting. For this, Malala is known as the schoolgirl who defied terrorists, working to combat their hatred with education and peace.

Newspapers around the world reported on the Taliban's attack on Malala.

Malala received the Nobel Peace Prize in 2014.

John Bul Dau

Journey of a Lost Boy

More than 20,000 boys were running for their lives from a civil war in Sudan, in East Africa. Fleeing their homes on foot, they set out on a perilous journey across the Sahara Desert. Government-backed troops in Sudan were after them, determined to annihilate the Christian population in the southern part of the country. The young boys became known around the world as the "Lost Boys." And John Bul Dau was one of them.

A Harrowing Escape

John was born Dhieu-Deng Leek on January 15, 1974, into the Dinka tribe. The Dinka people are from Sudan, in East Africa. John's life was that of a typical Sudanese boy, and he lived with his parents and siblings in their village. All of this changed when Sudan plunged into a civil war between the Muslim north and the Christian south. Thousands of people fled from their homes and villages, causing a monumental refugee crisis.

The night he was forced to leave home in 1987, John had trouble falling asleep in the sticky heat of the children's hut. After a brief moment of sudden whistling and tree branches cracking in the forest, the dark night lit up with explosions. Raiders, called the *djellabas,* set huts ablaze. They killed men, captured women and girls, and then proceeded to destroy the village.

In the chaos, John lost track of his family. A man whom John had mistaken for his father saved his life by grabbing him, hiding him, and forcing him to remain silent as the killers passed. Luckily, the armed men did not catch sight of John.

That night, John made a brave escape from his ravaged home. The 13-year-old had no clothes, no shoes, no food or water, and no family members with him. He was one of thousands of boys who fled Sudan during the war between 1983 and 2005. The boys, ranging in age from 3 to 13, walked across Sudan to seek

40

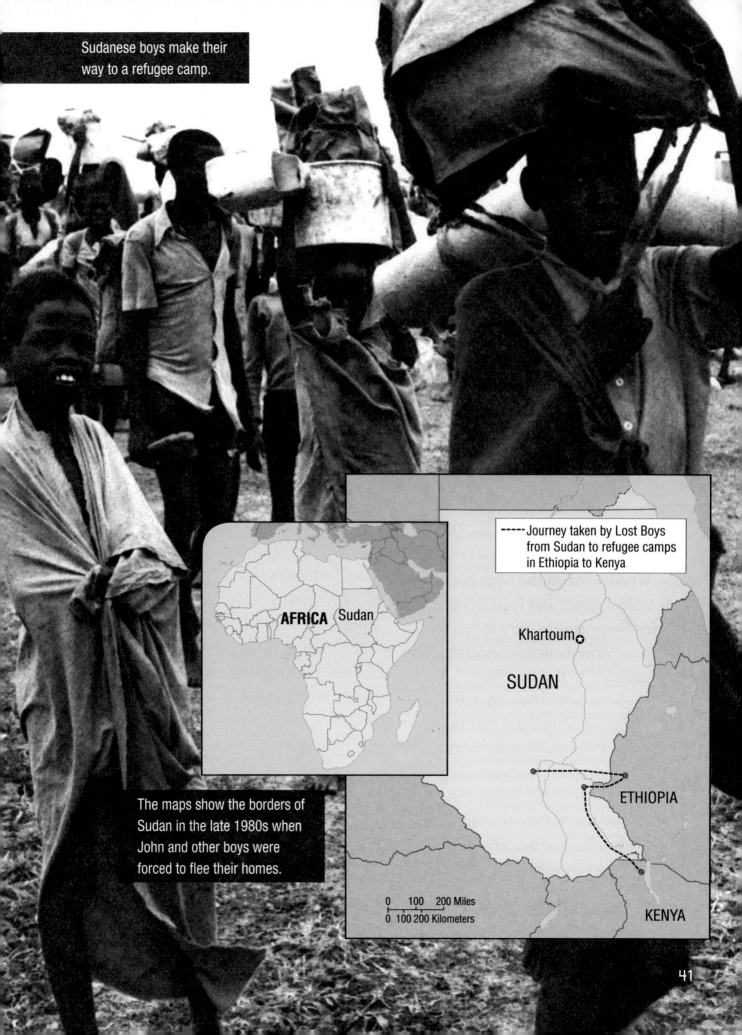

Sudanese boys make their way to a refugee camp.

------ Journey taken by Lost Boys from Sudan to refugee camps in Ethiopia to Kenya

AFRICA Sudan

Khartoum ✪

SUDAN

ETHIOPIA

KENYA

The maps show the borders of Sudan in the late 1980s when John and other boys were forced to flee their homes.

0   100   200 Miles
0 100 200 Kilometers

refuge in the neighboring countries of Ethiopia and Kenya. The terrifying thousand-mile trek lasted for months. Survival seemed impossible and, for many, it was. Thousands of boys died from starvation, dehydration, wild animal attacks, or disease. Once, when the rebels were shooting at them, some boys were forced to run into crocodile-infested waters as their only means of escape. Some of these boys were attacked by crocodiles, and others drowned.

The Struggle to Stay Alive

John was a natural leader, and being unusually tall and one of the older boys, he bravely assumed the role of caretaker for the younger ones. John searched for water in the desert for days. When some of the boys perished from lack of water and food, John dug shallow graves to bury them. He himself collapsed once, wondering if he would make it to the next day.

Out of the more than 20,000 boys that fled Sudan, roughly 4,000 made it out alive. Eventually, most of the survivors arrived at a refugee camp in Ethiopia. When that camp was attacked, however, they traveled for months again to northern Kenya. John lived in a Kenyan refugee camp for more than ten years, attending school for the first time and learning to write with sticks in the dirt.

Upon learning of the refugee crisis, churches and organizations in the United States decided to sponsor Sudanese refugees. John was among the lucky ones who would start a new life in America.

Looking Forward to Giving Back

By 2001, John had spent more than half of his 27 years in forced exile, but he was finally starting a new life in Syracuse, New York, where the winters were as cold as the climate in Sudan was hot. John had gone from one extreme to another, but it didn't matter to him because he was alive. Other Lost Boys, now young men, made new homes in various states across the country.

In America, John worked diligently, enrolling in college courses and working three jobs to earn enough money for his living expenses. John never forgot about those he left behind in Africa and managed to send some of his money to the friends who remained at the refugee camp in Kenya.

About a decade after he fled Sudan, John learned that his mother and a sister were alive at a refugee camp in Uganda. With money he had saved and help from the International Red Cross, he succeeded in bringing them to America.

The civil war in Sudan led to a division that resulted in the independence of South Sudan. Both countries continue to struggle with ongoing violence. John's only wish is for the people of his country to thrive. He continues to work toward this dream through the John Dau Foundation, an organization he established to help build clinics and schools in his home country. In May 2007, the first clinic opened. It has since provided life-saving medical care to more than 75,000 people.

John married another Sudanese refugee, and he now has children of his own. He continues to believe in the importance of facing obstacles with courage, even when the odds are stacked against him. This strength of character is one he hopes to pass on to his children.

John places plaster and paper bones on the National Mall in Washington, D.C., in 2013 to help raise awareness of genocide and mass murder.

Bill of Rights

On September 25, 1789, the U.S. Congress sent the state legislatures twelve proposed amendments to the Constitution. Ten of these amendments were ratified by the states and became law on December 15, 1791. These first ten amendments to the Constitution are known collectively as the Bill of Rights, and they explicitly protect the basic principles of liberty that critics of the Constitution argued were missing from the document.

AMENDMENT

I Congress shall make no law respecting an establishment of religion, or prohibiting the free exercise thereof; or abridging the freedom of speech, or of the press; or the right of the people peaceably to assemble, and to petition the government for a redress of grievances.

AMENDMENT

II A well-regulated militia, being necessary to the security of a free state, the right of the people to keep and bear arms, shall not be infringed.

AMENDMENT

III No soldier shall, in time of peace be quartered in any house, without the consent of the owner, nor in time of war, but in a manner to be prescribed by law.

AMENDMENT

IV The right of the people to be secure in their persons, houses, papers, and effects, against unreasonable searches and seizures, shall not be violated, and no warrants shall issue, but upon probable cause, supported by oath or affirmation, and particularly describing the place to be searched, and the persons or things to be seized.

AMENDMENT V

No person shall be held to answer for a capital, or otherwise infamous crime, unless on a presentment or indictment of a grand jury, except in cases arising in the land or naval forces, or in the militia, when in actual service in time of war or public danger; nor shall any person be subject for the same offense to be twice put in jeopardy of life or limb; nor shall be compelled in any criminal case to be a witness against himself, nor be deprived of life, liberty, or property, without due process of law; nor shall private property be taken for public use, without just compensation.

AMENDMENT VI

In all criminal prosecutions, the accused shall enjoy the right to a speedy and public trial, by an impartial jury of the state and district wherein the crime shall have been committed, which district shall have been previously ascertained by law, and to be informed of the nature and cause of the accusation; to be confronted with the witnesses against him; to have compulsory process for obtaining witnesses in his favor, and to have the assistance of counsel for his defense.

AMENDMENT VII

In suits at common law, where the value in controversy shall exceed twenty dollars, the right of trial by jury shall be preserved, and no fact tried by a jury, shall be otherwise reexamined in any court of the United States, than according to the rules of the common law.

AMENDMENT VIII

Excessive bail shall not be required, nor excessive fines imposed, nor cruel and unusual punishments inflicted.

AMENDMENT IX

The enumeration in the Constitution, of certain rights, shall not be construed to deny or disparage others retained by the people.

AMENDMENT X

The powers not delegated to the United States by the Constitution, nor prohibited by it to the states, are reserved to the states respectively, or to the people.

NO VACANCY

When an African-American boy arrives at an elite New England boarding school to run track in 1938, he faces the cold, hard facts of discrimination—and resolves to overcome it . . .

written by Katherine Carlman
illustrated by Susan Keeter
reprinted with the permission of *Plays, The Drama Magazine for Young People*

CHARACTERS

MISS SPARROW, white woman, early 20s

MRS. LEACH, white woman, mid-50s

LEWIS CROMWELL IV, white male, about 15

RAYMOND MCGRATH, African-American male, 14

COACH LOVSHIN, white male, late 20s

Though this play is based on actual events reported on Phillips Exeter Academy's website about racial discrimination that occurred at the school in 1938, all characters (except for Coach Lovshin, who was actually the Phillips Exeter coach), actions, and conversations are the creation of the author.

SCENE ONE

TIME: *1938.*

SETTING: *Main office of Phillips Exeter Academy, a private school in New Hampshire. There are two office desks with chairs, a file cabinet, two visitor chairs. Typewriters, papers, file folders, other items are on desks. One desk also has a telephone on it.*

AT RISE: *MRS. LEACH sits at her desk, working—typing, stuffing envelopes, etc. MISS SPARROW is assisting LEWIS CROMWELL IV.*

LEWIS CROMWELL IV *(Handing check over):* All I know is that my father's—Mr. Lewis Cromwell the third's—secretary instructed me to give this check to you.

MISS SPARROW *(Tentative):* But parents usually send payment via wire.

MRS. LEACH *(Looking up):* That will be fine, Miss Sparrow.

LEWIS *(To MISS SPARROW):* Do you mind calculating it again?

MISS SPARROW: Not at all, Mr. Cromwell. *(As MISS SPARROW tabulates amounts, telephone rings, and MRS. LEACH answers it.)*

MRS. LEACH *(Into phone):* Phillips Exeter Academy, may I help you? . . . Yes, classes start first thing in the morning. Convocation is at eight o'clock. . . . Yes. . . . Thank you. Goodbye. *(Hangs up. RAYMOND MCGRATH enters, carrying two battered suitcases, stands behind LEWIS.)*

MISS SPARROW *(Finishing her calculation):* So, Mr. Cromwell, that will be six hundred and forty—

LEWIS: My father's secretary made the check out for five hundred and twenty dollars. *(MISS SPARROW looks at MRS. LEACH, who nods.)*

MISS SPARROW *(Taking check):* Yes, Mr. Cromwell. Thank you, sir. You can go directly to Abbot Hall, room 412.

LEWIS *(Triumphantly):* Thank you. *(LEWIS exits, looking at RAYMOND as he passes. RAYMOND pushes his bags a bit closer to MISS SPARROW's desk.)*

MISS SPARROW *(To RAYMOND):* May I help you?

RAYMOND: Hi, I'm Ray McGrath. *(RAYMOND reaches out to shake MISS SPARROW's hand. MISS SPARROW extends her hand, looks over at MRS. LEACH, who raises her eyebrows.)* I'm here to get my room assignment.

MISS SPARROW: Room assignment?

RAYMOND *(Full of confidence):* Yes, ma'am. *(MISS SPARROW goes over to filing cabinet, pulls a file.)*

MISS SPARROW: Here we are. Raymond McGrath.

RAYMOND *(Smiling):* Yes, ma'am!

MISS SPARROW: Your tuition is paid in full. *(After a beat)* You do not owe us any money.

RAYMOND: Right! Right, I'm on scholarship for track, but I just don't know which dorm I'm in. I need my room number.

MISS SPARROW *(Tentative):* Yes, you have a tuition scholarship, that's correct, but . . . there's no charge on your bill for room and board. *(RAYMOND looks at her cautiously, frowning. He knows something's not right, but he's not sure what it is. He realizes he must be careful as he proceeds.)*

RAYMOND: Can you show me my bill?

MISS SPARROW: Certainly. *(MISS SPARROW hands RAYMOND his bill; he reviews it.)*

RAYMOND: This just says, "Scholarship Boy."

MISS SPARROW: Indeed, we have no record of a tuition bill for you because you're receiving a scholarship.

RAYMOND: Why aren't my room and board on this bill? (MISS SPARROW looks over to MRS. LEACH, who gets up and approaches RAYMOND.)

MRS. LEACH: Hello, there, I'm Mrs. Leach. How are you?

RAYMOND: I'm fine, Mrs. Leach. I just don't know where I'm gonna sleep tonight. (Gesturing to suitcases) Where do I go to unpack my bags?

MRS. LEACH (Leaning in, speaking low): Certainly, Raymond, you understand the (Awkwardly) situation.

RAYMOND (Getting upset): Raymond? That other boy was "Mr. Cromwell," but I'm "Raymond"? (In a moment of realization) Oh-h-h. There's no "mistake," is there? (MRS. LEACH shakes her head.) I've been accepted as a student— I'm expected to run for Phillips Exeter— but I don't get a room? (MRS. LEACH nods her head. MISS SPARROW looks down. RAYMOND draws himself to full height.) Yeah, I understand the situation. (He picks up his bags and starts to exit.)

MRS. LEACH: Raymond, where are you going?

RAYMOND: It's Mr. McGrath, and I'm going to talk to Coach Lovshin! (Curtain)

SCENE TWO

TIME: A few minutes later.

SETTING: Coach Lovshin's office, with desk and chair. Working door is right. Cabinet, two additional chairs for guests, running equipment piled here or there. A couple of trophies on desk or cabinet. Pennants on the walls.

AT RISE: The office door is open. COACH LOVSHIN is at his desk, reading a newspaper, when RAYMOND approaches and knocks on open door. He remains in the doorway without entering, still holding both suitcases. COACH puts down his paper.

COACH: Raymond! It's good to see you! Welcome to Phillips Exeter.

RAYMOND (Upset): Coach Lovshin, I'm going home!

COACH (Springing up): What? Raymond, wait a minute. What do you mean?

RAYMOND: Those ladies in the office— they won't give me a room! (COACH is silent, drops his head a bit.) Is that it? Is that all you're going to do? Hang your head? Because if it is, I'm going home. (COACH is silent, looking at RAYMOND.) Can't you hear me? I said "I - going - home!" (RAYMOND turns to exit, calls back.) I didn't come up to this school so they could treat me like this! You never told my mama they were going to do this to me!

COACH (*Advancing toward RAYMOND*): Raymond, please . . . let's talk about it. Come in, sit down. (*RAYMOND turns toward COACH, but doesn't put bags down.*) No? How about just putting the bags down? They must be heavy. (*RAYMOND stares at COACH; grips bags more tightly*) O.K., O.K., you don't have to move or do anything you don't want to do. But can we talk before you head off?

RAYMOND: Start talking. (*COACH heads back into his office.*)

COACH: So let me ask you, Raymond, when I first came to recruit you, what if I had said to you, "Come run for Phillips Exeter, but you won't have a place to rest your head"? (*RAYMOND is silent.*) What if, after I scouted you and talked to your mother—what if I'd said, "By the way, Mrs. McGrath, they'll give your son a scholarship so he can run track for them, but they won't let him stay in the dormitory with white boys"? (*RAYMOND slams his bags to the ground, advances into office.*)

RAYMOND (*Angrily*): She would've asked you to get out of her house!

COACH (*Calmly*): And she would've been right to do so.

RAYMOND: YOU TRICKED ME! *And* my mother!

COACH (*Calmly*): No.

RAYMOND (*Stepping closer to COACH*): You knew they'd do this to me!

COACH: No. I didn't know. (*After a beat*) I was afraid, yes, but I was hopeful, too. Come on, sit down. Hear me out. (*RAYMOND grudgingly sits.*) Look, if they've gotten to the point that they're accepting students . . . like you—

RAYMOND (*Rising*): That's it. I'm going home!

COACH: Raymond—don't.

RAYMOND: Why not? You can't even say I'm colored! What's wrong with this place? Give me one good reason why I shouldn't catch the next bus home!

COACH: Tell me something . . . why did you come here in the first place?

RAYMOND: To run track.

COACH: You could've run track at the Hopewell School for Colored Boys back in Alabama, couldn't you?

RAYMOND: Yes, and that's right where I'll be heading now.

COACH: But you didn't choose to go there in the first place. Why? (*Louder, to get RAYMOND's attention*) Why did you decide to come to Phillips Exeter, Raymond?

RAYMOND (*Flustered*): For an education!

COACH: And why did you want to get that education here?

RAYMOND (*Frustrated*): Stop asking me so many questions! (*RAYMOND gets up, walks toward door.*)

COACH: Don't run away! (*RAYMOND stops, turns to face COACH.*)

RAYMOND: You tell me—you tell me why you let me come up here knowing they might treat me like this.

COACH: Because I believe in you!

RAYMOND: Well, that still doesn't answer my question—or get me a place to sleep here.

COACH (Calmly): Getting an education at Phillips Exeter is the best thing you can do for yourself—for your future and for your family. Students who graduate with good grades from this school go to the best colleges in the country—can you imagine that?

RAYMOND: I don't need Phillips Exeter to go to college!

COACH: You do if you want to get into an Ivy League school! Don't you see the potential, Raymond? With your brains and your abilities as a sprinter? You could go to Harvard!

RAYMOND: Why should I go to all that trouble? Work hard here and put up with this garbage just so I can go to some fancy white college where they're gonna deny me a room, too?!

COACH: You don't know that.

RAYMOND: You think going without a room will help me? You want me to go from fancy school to fancy school, making everybody impressed, but never having a bed? Nah, I'm going home! (RAYMOND moves to pick up his luggage.)

COACH: You think it's just you, don't you? *(RAYMOND stops, turns.)*

RAYMOND: What do you mean?

COACH: You're not our first colored student, you know. You think the few fellows that they've let in before you haven't gone through the same thing?

RAYMOND *(Surprised):* There are other colored students here?

COACH: They graduated. One's in medical school in New Jersey. The other opened a chemical research business in New York. *(Shrugs)* You've got to start somewhere, right? I remember when Phillips Exeter only accepted white boys, but—things are changing!

RAYMOND: But where did those other guys sleep?

COACH: Off campus. In a boarding house. In the back room at a tailor's shop.

RAYMOND: No. I don't want that! I'm not going to sleep in some back room. I'm getting something better for myself in this life!

COACH: Better than a great education? Listen to me. So, O.K., your pride's hurt. But if you can suffer this humiliation, you'll rise to a higher level! Believe me, I know.

RAYMOND: How do you know, Coach Lovshin? YOU'RE WHITE! You don't know! How do you think you can tell me you know?

COACH: I'm a coach here, Raymond.

RAYMOND *(Frowning):* I know that!

COACH: And I have a Ph.D. in education. You know that, too? Or do you think I'm just some guy who can make boys run?

RAYMOND *(Amazed):* You have a Ph.D.? Then why aren't you a teacher?

COACH *(Shrugging):* I'm Catholic. And Phillips Exeter doesn't hire Catholics onto their faculty—yet.

RAYMOND: And you're just going to wait around until they do? You could be a faculty member at another school. You could be making a lot of money!

COACH: My family is here. All my siblings and my parents. My wife and kids have their friends and family. Besides, in some small way, I feel I'm fighting a good fight. *(RAYMOND sighs, looks away.)* You know the student I told you about? The one in medical school? What if he had left that first day? What if he just walked out the door when he found out he wouldn't be allowed to live in the dorm? *(After a pause)* Doesn't someone have to be the one to go first? Maybe it takes two or three tries—maybe twenty—but doesn't someone have to charge in and break down barriers? If we aren't willing to fight for what's right, things'll never change, Raymond.

RAYMOND *(Looking at COACH, shaking his head):* You're crazy.

COACH: Maybe.

RAYMOND: You could teach at some other school and be respected!

COACH: And what would I accomplish? Other than making money and feeling comfortable? Some things are more important. If we can make things better for people who come after us . . . well, I think that's an important thing to do. *(COACH moves to pick up RAYMOND's bags.)* Look, don't give up—don't be a quitter. Take your classes, run track— and succeed! *(COACH picks up the first bag, brushes it off.)* What do you say? You can have a room at my house, Raymond. My wife's a good cook, and my kids don't make too much noise. *(RAYMOND raises his eyebrow as COACH picks up the other bag.)* O.K, O.K., maybe I've just gotten used to the noise. You will, too, before too long. Come, stay with us. C'mon. *(COACH motions for RAYMOND to come with him. After a beat, RAYMOND moves toward COACH. When he reaches him, he tries to take a bag from him. COACH resists for a moment, still worried RAYMOND will leave.)*

RAYMOND: It's O.K., Coach, I'm not gonna run away. *(COACH relinquishes one bag. They exchange a look of understanding. COACH gives RAYMOND a nod, and the two exit as curtain closes.)*

THE END

PRODUCTION NOTES

CHARACTERS: 3 male, 2 female.

PLAYING TIME: Approximately 10 minutes.

COSTUMES: Representative of the time. Secretary and Mrs. Leach are in professional business attire. Lewis Cromwell IV wears dress pants and buttoned shirt with a sweater around his shoulders. Raymond wears a suit. Coach wears a track suit.

PROPERTIES: Two battered suitcases.

SETTING: Scene One, Main office of Phillips Exeter Academy, a private school in New Hampshire. There are two office desks with chairs, a file cabinet, two visitor chairs. Typewriters, papers, file folders, other items are on desks. One desk also has telephone on it. Scene Two, Coach Lovshin's office, with desk and chair. Working door is right. Cabinet, two additional chairs for guests, running equipment piled here or there. A couple of trophies on desk or cabinet. Pennants on the walls.

LIGHTING: No special effects.

SOUND: Ringing telephone.

Our March to Freedom Is Irreversible

Excerpt from a speech by Nelson Mandela

Nelson Mandela (right) in 1958

In 1964, Nelson Mandela was charged with sabotage against the South African government. He would spend almost 27 years of his life behind bars. Upon his release from prison on February 11, 1990, Mandela addressed a crowd that had amassed to greet him in Cape Town.

Friends, comrades, and fellow South Africans, I greet you all in the name of peace, democracy, and freedom for all. I stand here before you not as a prophet but as a humble servant of you, the people.

Your tireless and heroic sacrifices have made it possible for me to be here today. I, therefore, place the remaining years of my life in your hands.

On this day of my release I extend my sincere and warmest gratitude to the millions of my compatriots and those in every corner of the globe who have campaigned tirelessly for my release.

I extend special greetings to the people of Cape Town. This city to which, which has been my home for three decades.*

Your mass marches, and other forms of struggle, have served as a constant source of strength to all political prisoners. . . .

I extend my greetings to the working class of our country. Your organised strength is the pride of our movement. You remain the most dependable force in the struggle to end exploitation and oppression. . . .

I pay tribute to the endless heroism of the youth. You, the young lions, you, the young lions, have energised our entire struggle.

I pay tribute to the mothers and wives and sisters of our nation. You are the rock-hard foundation of our struggle. Apartheid has inflicted more pain on you than on anyone else.

On this occasion, we thank the world, we thank the world community for their great contribution to the anti-apartheid struggle. Without your support, our struggle would not have reached this advanced stage. The sacrifice of the front line states will be remembered by South Africans forever. . . .

Today, the majority of South Africans, black and white, recognise that apartheid has no future. It has to be ended by our own decisive mass action in order to build peace and security. The mass campaigns of defiance, and other actions of our organisations and people, can only culminate in the establishment of democracy.

The apartheid destruction on our subcontinent is incalculable. The fabric of family life of millions of my people has been shattered. Millions are homeless and unemployed. Our economy, our economy lies in ruins and our people are embroiled in political strife. . . .

The need to unite the people of our country is as important a task now as it always has been. No individual leader is able to take on these enormous tasks on his own.

It is our task as leaders to place our views before our organisation and to allow the democratic structures to decide on the way forward. On the question of democratic practice, I feel duty bound to make the point that a leader of the movement is the person who has been democratically elected at a national

*Speech is reproduced here exactly as delivered, including some words and phrases that were repeated.

our *free*dom

conference. This is the principle which must be upheld without any exception. . . .

It is our belief that the future of our country can only be determined by a body which is democratically elected on a non-racial basis.

Negotiations on the dismantling of apartheid will have to address the overwhelming demands of our people for a democratic, non-racial, and unitary South Africa.

There must be an end to white monopoly on political power, and a fundamental restructuring of our political and economic systems to ensure that the inequalities of apartheid are addressed and our society thoroughly democratised. . . .

Our struggle has reached a decisive moment. We call on our people to seize this moment so that the process towards democracy is rapid and uninterrupted.

We have waited too long for our freedom. We can no longer wait. Now is the time to intensify the struggle on all fronts. To relax our efforts now would be a mistake which generations to come will not be able to forgive.

The sight of freedom looming on the horizon should encourage us to redouble our efforts. It is only through disciplined mass action that our victory can be assured.

We call on our white compatriots to join us in the shaping of a new South Africa. The freedom movement is a political home for you too. We call on the international community to continue the campaign to isolate the apartheid regime.

To lift sanctions now would be to run the risk of aborting the process towards the complete eradication of apartheid. Our march to freedom is irreversible. We must not allow fear to stand in our way.

Universal suffrage on a common voters' role in united democratic and non-racial South Africa is the only way to peace and racial harmony.

In conclusion, I wish to quote my own words during my trial in 1964. They are as true today as they were then. I quote:

"I have fought against white domination and I have fought against black domination. I have cherished the ideal of a democratic and free society in which all persons live together in harmony and with equal opportunities. It is an ideal which I hope to live for and to achieve. But, if needs be, it is an ideal for which I am prepared to die."

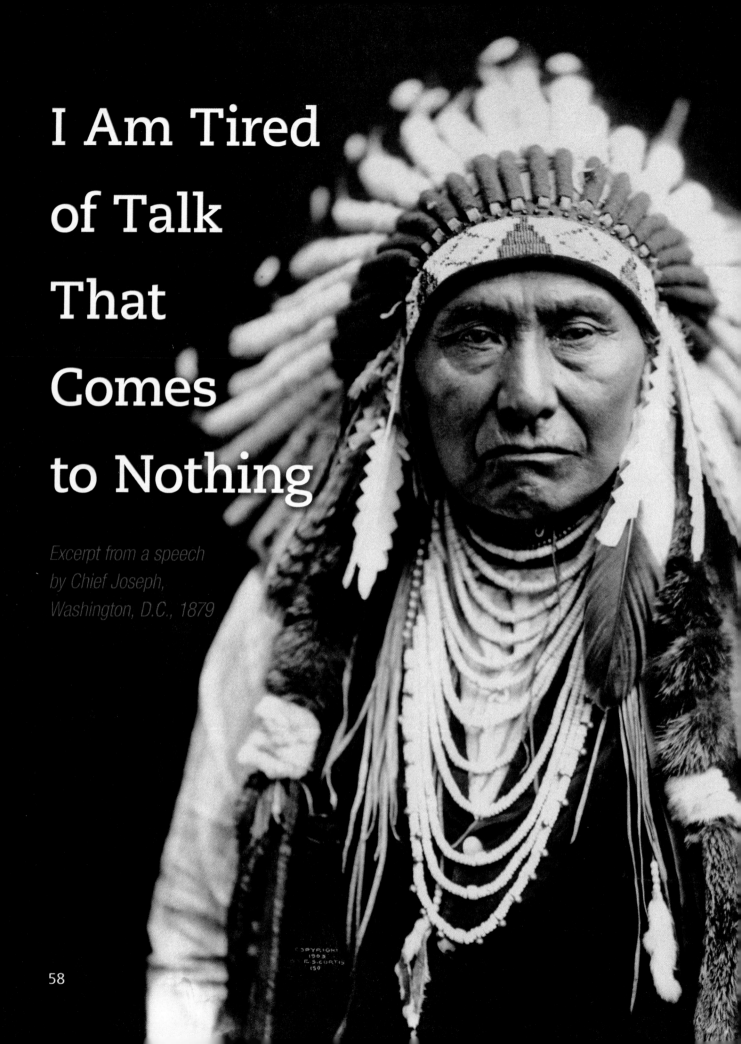

I Am Tired of Talk That Comes to Nothing

Excerpt from a speech by Chief Joseph, Washington, D.C., 1879

I am tired of talk that comes to nothing. It makes my heart sick when I remember all the good words and all the broken promises. There has been too much talking by men who had no right to talk. Too many misinterpretations have been made; too many misunderstandings have come up between the white men and the Indians. If the white man wants to live in peace with the Indian he can live in peace. There need be no trouble. Treat all men alike. Give them the same laws. Give them all an even chance to live and grow. All men were made by the same Great Spirit Chief. They are all brothers. The earth is the mother of all people, and all people should have equal rights upon it. You might as well expect all rivers to run backward as that any man who was born a free man should be contented penned up and denied liberty to go where he pleases. If you tie a horse to a stake, do you expect he will grow fat? If you pen an Indian up on a small spot of earth and compel him to stay there, he will not be contented nor will he grow and prosper. I have asked some of the Great White Chiefs where they get their authority to say to the Indian that he shall stay in one place, while he sees white men going where they please. They cannot tell me. . . .

When I think of our condition, my heart is heavy. I see men of my own race treated as outlaws and driven from country to country, or shot down like animals.

I know that my race must change. We cannot hold our own with the white men as we are. We only ask an even chance to live as other men live. We ask to be recognized as men. We ask that the same law shall work alike on all men. If an Indian breaks the law, punish him by the law. If a white man breaks the law, punish him also.

Let me be a free man, free to travel, free to stop, free to work, free to trade where I choose, free to choose my own teachers, free to follow the religion of my fathers, free to talk, think and act for myself—and I will obey every law or submit to the penalty.

Whenever the white man treats the Indian as they treat each other then we shall have no more wars. We shall be all alike—brothers of one father and mother, with one sky above us and one country around us and one government for all. Then the Great Spirit Chief who rules above will smile upon this land and send rain to wash out the bloody spots made by brothers' hands upon the face of the earth. For this time the Indian race is waiting and praying. I hope no more groans of wounded men and women will ever go to the ear of the Great Spirit Chief above, and that all people may be one people.

GADGETS
AND GAMES

BY CHRIS OXLADE

CONTENTS

Some words are shown in bold, **like this.**
You can find out what they mean by looking
in the glossary.

GADGETS, GAMES, AND LIFE CYCLES

Gadgets are part of our everyday lives. The most popular gadgets include cell phones, **smartphones** (such as the iPhone® and BlackBerry® phones), MP3 players, tablets (for example, the iPad®), and e-book readers (such as the Kindle®). In this book, we also look at video game consoles, such as the Xbox® and PlayStation®. Have you ever wondered how these gadgets are made?

All gadgets are made up of hardware (their physical parts) and **software**. A gadget needs software called an **operating system** (such as iOS®) that controls the parts of the gadget itself. It also needs programs or **applications** ("apps" for short), which make it do different jobs, such as e-mailing and browsing the Internet. Games for computers, video game consoles, tablets, and smartphones are applications.

Gadget life cycles

All gadgets have life cycles. The cycle begins with the initial idea for the gadget and ends when it is no longer used. In between these come **designing**, making **prototypes**, **manufacturing**, **marketing** and selling, maintaining, and finally reusing, **recycling**, or disposing. The life cycle of some gadgets, such as smartphones, is very short—it might be just a couple of years. This is because many people replace their phones every year or so.

LIFE CYCLE PEOPLE

Many people are involved in the life cycle of a gadget. They include designers and engineers, as well as the people who assemble and sell the product. Designers and engineers work on the design, prototyping, and manufacturing parts of a **product life cycle**, which is called the **engineering** life cycle.

Designers and engineers often invent new **technologies,** which are then used in gadgets. They also improve technology that already exists, to make gadgets better or cheaper.

Gadgets old and new

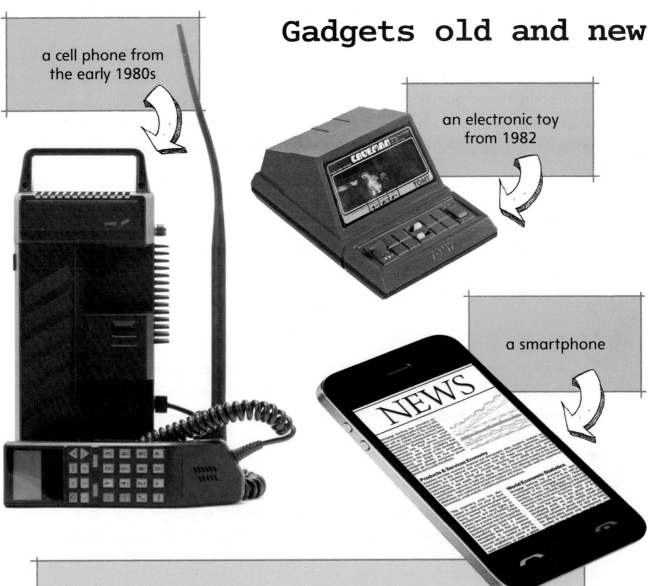

a cell phone from the early 1980s

an electronic toy from 1982

a smartphone

CONTRAST THE PAST

The smartphones, video game consoles, MP3 players, and tablets we have today are very different from the first electronic gadgets. This is evidence for how quickly technology has changed. The first hand-held cell phones appeared in the 1970s. They were the size of a brick, and almost as heavy! They also only made phone calls.

Modern smartphones are really compact computers, with the power that desktop personal computers had just a decade ago. Miniaturization (see page 75) of electronics has been one factor in this change. The first computer game consoles also appeared in the 1970s. They allowed you to play very simple, two-dimensional (2-D) tennis games. Modern consoles have enormous power by comparison, with the ability to display incredibly detailed three-dimensional (3-D) graphics.

Important terms

There are many terms and concepts that are used in the world of design, engineering, and technology. They are also referred to as we look at the life cycle of gadgets and games. Knowing these terms and concepts will help you to understand all product life cycles, not just those of gadgets and games. The terms are summarized here so you can refer back to them when you need to.

Product life cycle

A product life cycle refers to the series of events in the life of a gadget. It starts with the initial idea and ends with disposal or recycling. The life cycle includes design, prototyping, manufacturing, and marketing.

Design

Design involves the process of choosing materials, **components,** and the appearance of a gadget, taking into account **requirements** and **constraints** in a design brief. **Software design** is figuring out how software for gadgets and games will work.

Requirements

Requirements are the features and characteristics a gadget must have (such as speed, memory size, or battery life). Requirements are written in a design brief.

Constraints

Constraints are the limits the designers have to work within (such as budget and size). Constraints are written in a design brief.

System

A **system** is a set of things that work together to do a job. A system has an **input**, a **process**, and an **output**. Information of some sort goes into the system through the input, is processed, and then goes to an output.

Prototype

A prototype is a test version, made before the gadget goes into production, to make sure it can be made and works properly.

Engineering

Engineering is using science and technology to design and make machines, structures, and devices. Electronic software and production engineering is particularly important in the design and manufacturing of gadgets.

Manufacturing

Manufacturing is the process of making products from materials and components. Gadgets are normally made by **mass production,** on **assembly lines.** Software DVDs and Blu-ray™ discs are made by batch production, where limited quantities of identical objects are made at the same time.

Computer-aided design and manufacturing

Computer-aided design (CAD) and **computer-aided manufacturing (CAM)** are the use of information and computer technology in the design and manufacturing of products.

Software

Software includes instructions and data that control what a gadget does. System software controls the parts of the gadget itself. Application software (an app) makes the gadget do a specific job.

Marketing

Marketing involves bringing a gadget to the attention of the consumer by advertising and holding product launches. Marketing also includes market research, which tries to find out what gadgets people want to buy.

Recycling

Recycling means using materials again. When a gadget reaches the end of its life cycle, it is recycled to reuse materials such as plastics and metals.

WHAT IS TECHNOLOGY?

Technology is modifying objects and materials to satisfy people's needs and wants. Technology can be as simple as a wooden stool and as complex as an **integrated circuit.**

THE LIFE CYCLE OF A TABLET

This flow chart shows the stages in the life cycle of a typical tablet, as an example of a gadget life cycle.

Initial idea

The first step in a tablet's life cycle is the initial idea, which comes from the manufacturer. The idea may come in response to consumer demand, or because the manufacturer has identified a new market. A design brief describes the requirements and constraints of the gadget.

Design

Working from a design brief, the designers choose materials and components and design the appearance, functions, and software. They write a design **specification** for the complete gadget.

End of life

Eventually, all gadgets become unused, outdated, or broken beyond repair. One of the following happens:

- Reusing: The tablet is given to another user, often after being refurbished.
- Recycling: The tablet is broken up and the materials inside are recycled. Some materials may be used as raw materials for new gadgets.
- Disposal: The tablet is thrown away.

Prototyping

A prototype is made to make sure the design works and that all the components fit and work together. Changes might be made to the design specification at this stage to solve any problems.

Materials

Extracting materials from the ground and processing them is part of the tablet's life cycle (for example, mining aluminum ore and processing it to extract the aluminum).

Manufacturing

Mass production is carried out on an assembly line. Components are added to the gadget until it is complete. Assembly starts with the circuit board. Electronic components are added to the board, then it is fitted into the case with other parts, such as the screen and connectors. The tablets are packaged, ready for sale.

Marketing

The manufacturer advertises on the Internet, on television, and in newspapers. The manufacturer holds a product launch party. Finished gadgets are distributed to retail stores and online sellers.

Useful life

Consumers buy the tablet. This stage is the **useful life** of the tablet. The tablet must be maintained throughout this period. Maintenance includes customer support, making spare parts, repairing flawed tablets, and releasing software updates.

WHAT IS THE NEED?

The life cycle of gadgets and games begins with an idea for a new product. Companies that manufacture these products want to make money. They will only spend money and time making them when they think there is a market for them. This means people want them and will probably buy them.

Market pull . . .

Consumers want gadgets because they are useful for communicating, for entertainment, for navigating, for reading e-books, and for work. Consumers want new games to play for entertainment and fun. This need from people is called consumer demand, or "market pull." Many people want the latest gadgets. These people create more demand, because they regularly buy new gadgets. Video game fans also want the latest games to play.

. . . and market push

Manufacturers also drive the need for new gadgets and games by manufacturing products they think consumers will want to buy. This is known as "market push." They might design a gadget with new features or that makes use of a new technology (such as a 3-D screen), or they might improve an existing gadget. They may also introduce new products in response to their rivals or update an existing product to extend its life cycle until a major new product is launched. Manufacturers always think about whether there is a gadget that does not exist that people will want—this is known as spotting a hole in the market.

MARKET RESEARCH

Manufacturers talk to people about their products. They ask them questions about which features they like, which ones they do not, and what they would like to use in the future. This is known as market research. Market researchers also look at sales figures to see which products are selling well and to look for holes in the market. Research helps manufacturers understand the latest trends in technology and how these might be relevant to them.

Uses of cell phones

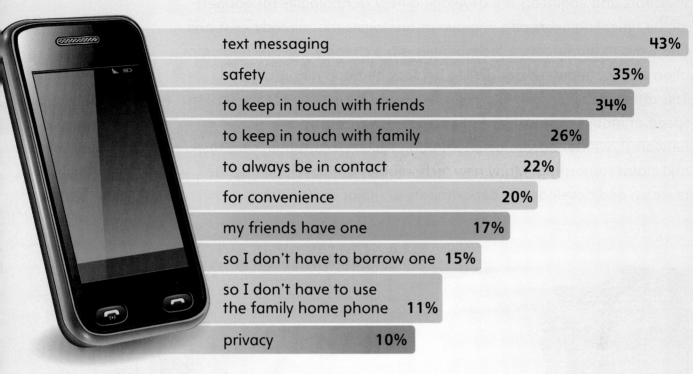

text messaging	43%
safety	35%
to keep in touch with friends	34%
to keep in touch with family	26%
to always be in contact	22%
for convenience	20%
my friends have one	17%
so I don't have to borrow one	15%
so I don't have to use the family home phone	11%
privacy	10%

This bar chart shows reasons for buying a cell phone as given by American teenagers in a 2010 poll.

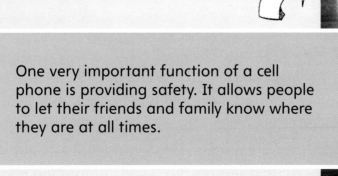

One very important function of a cell phone is providing safety. It allows people to let their friends and family know where they are at all times.

New technologies

Inventors and engineers are developing new technologies for gadgets all the time. Engineers also improve technologies that already exist and find ways to manufacture technologies more cheaply. New technologies allow new or improved gadgets to be designed and manufactured. This effect is called "technology push." Examples include the increasing speed of mobile data networks (such as the introduction of **4G** networks), which allow smartphones and tablets to communicate faster, and **cloud computing.** Many new technologies are developed by the research and development departments of major companies.

Since the success of the Nintendo Wii®, other manufacturers have developed their own motion control systems.

THE NINTENDO Wii

The Nintendo Wii was launched at the end of 2006. By the end of 2007, consumers around the world had bought 20 million units. By March 2011, 86 million Nintendo Wii units had been sold worldwide. The Wii's success was due mainly to its motion controllers. These contain sensors that send information about the position and angle of the controller to the console and allow players to control games with hand and arm movements.

Touch-screen displays, 3-D screens, motion sensors, lithium-ion batteries, digital compasses, face recognition, speech recognition, and wireless networking are all technologies that were once new, but are now common in modern gadgets. All these technologies make gadgets more useful and easier to use. New types of software developed for video games are also classed as new technology.

Technology push may also come from the need to reduce harm to the environment or to meet certain standards set by a country's laws. For example, solar-powered rechargers for gadgets and gadget batteries are a technology that reduces electricity consumption.

The new technologies used in gadgets are expensive to produce at first, so the gadgets that use them are expensive to buy. Prices gradually fall as the gadgets are made and sold in greater quantities. For example, the first touch-screen smartphones were expensive, but now even low-budget smartphones have touch screens.

LIFE CYCLE LENGTHS

The new technology in gadgets is developed very quickly. For example, more powerful processors are introduced every few months. This means some gadgets—especially cell phones—become out-of-date very quickly, often in just a few months. So, the life cycle of these gadgets is shorter than other products, such as televisions and cars.

WHAT HAVE WE LEARNED?

- The life cycle of a gadget begins with a need.
- Market pull is demand from consumers.
- Market push is created by manufacturers.
- Market research finds out what consumers want.
- New technologies allow new types of gadgets to be developed.

GADGET DESIGN

Once a gadget manufacturer has identified the need for a new gadget, the next step is to design it. The design stage is when an idea begins to be turned into a real product. Gadget designers are given a design brief that lists the requirements for a product and also the constraints.

This is a model for a new smartphone design.

REQUIREMENTS AND CONSTRAINTS

Requirements for a smartphone might be:

- the materials for the case
- screen size
- battery life
- resolution of the camera.

Constraints might be:

- the budget (how much the phone will cost to manufacture, which will limit the materials and components that the designers can choose)
- the maximum case size.

Manufacturers have to design a gadget's electronics, its software, and its shape, look, feel, and buttons. They employ designers from different disciplines (such as electronics designers, software designers, and artistic designers). The designers work from the design brief. They use their knowledge and experience of designing products in the past to design the new gadget.

Materials and components

Designers choose the materials a gadget will be made from. These will include plastics and metals for the structure, case, and buttons. Materials are chosen for their properties, such as strength, durability, color, and texture. For example, many handheld gadgets have a case made from polycarbonate, which is a very tough plastic, in case they are dropped. Designers also choose the components for gadgets, such as buttons, touch screens, and electronic components such as microprocessors and memory chips. The chosen materials and components form part of the design specification for a product. This contains all the information needed to manufacture the product.

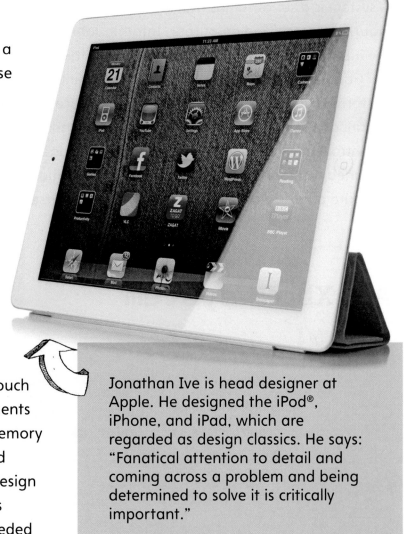

Jonathan Ive is head designer at Apple. He designed the iPod®, iPhone, and iPad, which are regarded as design classics. He says: "Fanatical attention to detail and coming across a problem and being determined to solve it is critically important."

ECO IMPACT

Gadgets use up energy throughout every stage in their life cycle. Much of it comes from burning fuels, which releases carbon dioxide and other greenhouse gases into the atmosphere. The amount of these gases released in the life cycle of a product is called its carbon footprint.

Recycled materials and energy efficiency reduce the carbon footprint of a gadget. For example, a Nokia 700® smartphone contains about 30 percent recycled materials and uses energy-saving technologies. It has a carbon footprint of 20 pounds (9 kilograms) of carbon dioxide. That is the same as the carbon footprint of 60 cans of soda.

Gadget systems

A system is a set of things that work together to do a job. A system has an input, a process, and an output. Information goes into the system through the input. It goes through a process, and it then goes to an output.

Gadgets have complex systems that continuously take inputs from buttons, touch screens, and microphones, process this information, and continuously send it to the screen, speakers, and other outputs. The system is controlled by software. All the parts of a gadget's system have to be designed. Sometimes designers take apart products from other manufacturers to figure out their systems. This is known as reverse engineering.

An Xbox system

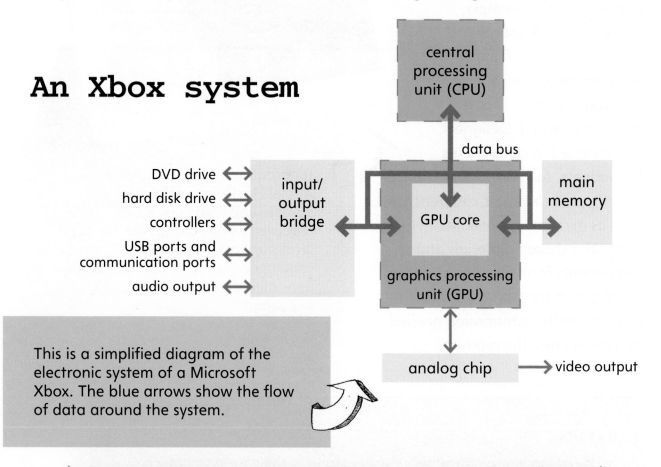

This is a simplified diagram of the electronic system of a Microsoft Xbox. The blue arrows show the flow of data around the system.

INTERFACE DESIGN

Part of designing a gadget's system is the interface between it and the user. For example, an e-book reader's system allows the user to flip from one page of a book to the next. The system of touches and swipes on the e-book reader's screen has to be designed, as does the way the pages of the book are displayed. Good interface design makes a gadget easy to operate.

Electronic design

Electronic designers design the complex electronic circuits inside gadgets. These are made up of circuit boards with components attached to them. The components include:

- buttons
- microphones
- speakers
- integrated circuits such as memory chips, microprocessors, and graphics controllers.

All these circuits are powered by a battery. Some new gadgets will use circuits from existing gadgets, and some will have circuits that are designed from scratch.

This integrated circuit is being designed on a computer.

MICROSCOPIC COMPONENTS

Every new generation of gadgets is faster and has more features than the previous generation. The power of software processors and the capacity and speed of memory chips increases from year to year. Designers are also able to squeeze the electronics into smaller spaces. This is because of the increasing miniaturization of components on integrated circuits. In modern integrated circuits, more than a million components can be squeezed into a single square millimeter.

There is a rule of thumb called "Moore's Law," thought up by the cofounder of the Intel company, Gordon E. Moore, that says the number of transistors placed inexpensively on an integrated circuit doubles approximately every two years. This has been adapted to say that the chip performance doubles approximately every 18 months.

Computers in design

Information and communications technology is an important tool. Working from a design specification, designers can draw the parts of gadgets on a computer. This is known as computer-aided design (CAD). Designers draw what the parts look like from the sides, from the ends, and from the top and bottom. The computer software builds up 3-D models that can be viewed on a screen. The parts can be displayed in "wire-frame," which means its shape is drawn with many polygons.

Models can also be displayed looking solid, in color, lit up from different directions, and with texture added. They can be tilted and turned and viewed from any angle. Realistic models are particularly useful for designing the appearance of a new gadget.

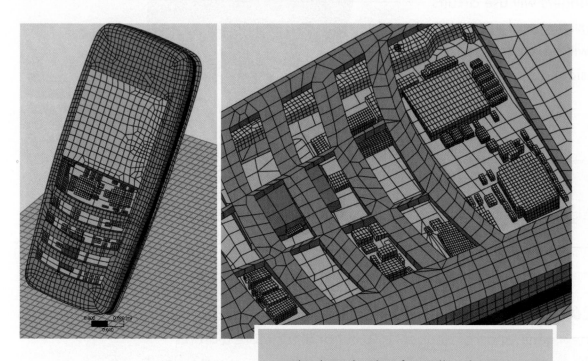

The hundreds of small polygons that make up the shape of this cell phone's parts can be seen in this wire-frame model.

Using CAD, designers can see how parts will look without having to actually make them. Shape, size, color, and texture can be adjusted. These models are eventually passed on for manufacturing real components (see page 88).

Virtual construction

CAD allows designers to build a model of the whole gadget, composed of models of each of the components. The software checks that different parts fit together, as if they were real objects. The parts can then be adjusted, if necessary. Building a computer model of the whole gadget means that many design problems are solved before a real prototype is made (see page 82).

Computer models of these cell phone components help to make sure the real physical parts will fit together.

Courtesy of iFixit.

Circuit design

Designers also use computers to design complex electronic circuits. Electronics designers build circuits from virtual components. They can see how the components will fit together physically and design the circuit boards that the components will be attached to. Using simulation software, designers can even test whether the circuits actually work.

Software design

Just as the physical parts of a gadget need to be designed, so does its software. Software design includes designing the operating system (including screen graphics such as icons and the user interface) and the applications, such as e-mail and mapping. Software design is part of software development, or the software development life cycle.

The first stage in the life cycle, which comes before the designers get to work, is to list requirements and constraints. These include the processing power and memory capacity of the gadget that the software will run on.

Software designers must think about the age and experience of the user. This will influence how they design it.

The design team

Dozens of designers are needed to design a complete operating system, so the work is divided up. Some designers will work on the user interface, others on the sound, and others on the communications (such as connecting to the Internet). The designers organize tasks into modules and write down what each module has to deliver. They do not actually write the software.

Software designers take into account who is going to use the software. For example, an application for young children will require a simple interface. Once the software is completely designed, it can be written, or implemented (see page 84). Games for personal computers, video game consoles, tablets, and smartphones go through a similar software development life cycle (see pages 80–81 for more on game design).

The software development process

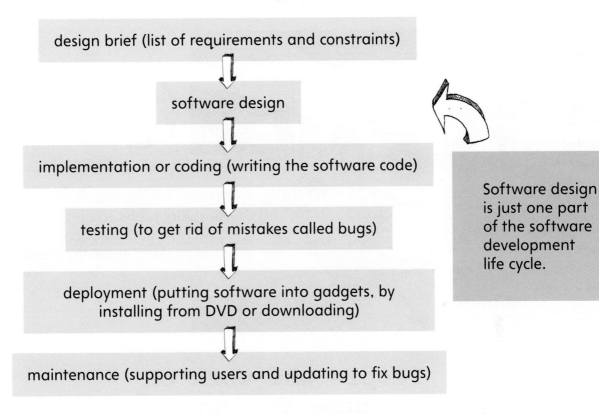

design brief (list of requirements and constraints)

software design

implementation or coding (writing the software code)

testing (to get rid of mistakes called bugs)

deployment (putting software into gadgets, by installing from DVD or downloading)

maintenance (supporting users and updating to fix bugs)

Software design is just one part of the software development life cycle.

CONTRAST THE PAST

Software on the first personal computers and video game consoles was very simple compared to today. This was mainly because computers and consoles had much slower and simpler processors and much less memory than modern computers and consoles. One good comparison is the size of applications. The applications for the Commodore 64™, a home computer of the mid-1980s, could be a maximum of 64 kilobytes in size. Today, even a simple application for a smartphone can be 100 megabytes or more in size. That is more than 1,000 times as large.

Game design

Producing games for personal computers, smartphones, tablets, and video game consoles is called game development. The first stage in game development is game design. Once a game developer has decided what genre of game to develop (adventure, simulation, strategy, puzzle, and so on) and decided on the subject of the game, the game can be designed.

Game design depends on the platform (the gadget, console, or computer) the game will be played on. Some games are released for several platforms, and so a slightly different design is needed for each one.

This game designer is using a graphics tablet to manipulate onscreen objects. He has an artist's sketchbook for reference.

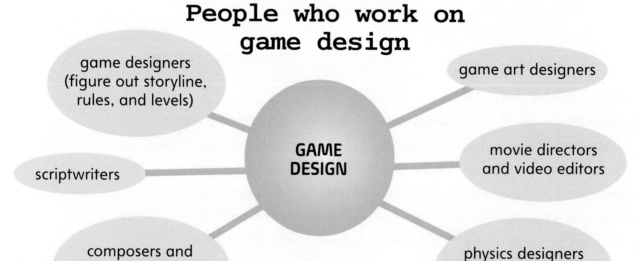

People who work on game design

game designers (figure out storyline, rules, and levels)

game art designers

scriptwriters

GAME DESIGN

movie directors and video editors

composers and experts in music and sound production

physics designers (figure out how objects move and interact)

Complex games

Development of the driving game Gran Turismo™ took five years.

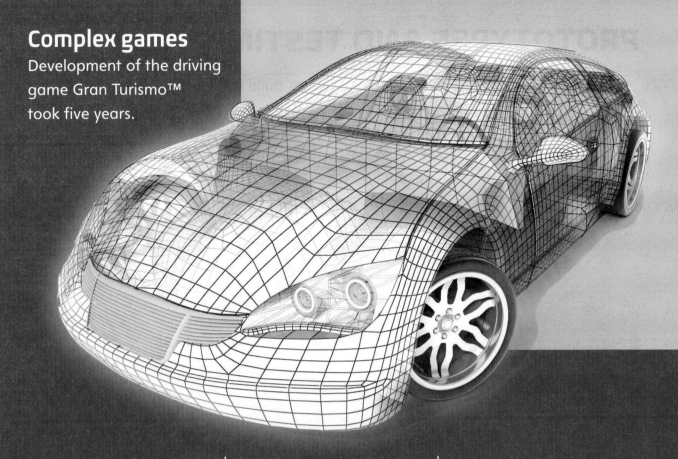

DESIGNERS CREATED SUPER-REALISTIC MODELS OF **1,000** REAL CARS FOR PLAYERS TO "DRIVE."

SOME CARS WERE CREATED USING UP TO **500,000** POLYGONS TO REPRESENT THEIR SURFACES. THE DESIGNS MIGHT HAVE LOOKED SIMILAR TO THE DIAGRAM ABOVE.

THE GAME COST OVER **$80 MILLION** TO PRODUCE.

WHAT HAVE WE LEARNED?
- A design brief is a list of requirements and constraints.
- Designers choose materials and components.
- A system has inputs, processes, and outputs.
- ICT is used widely in product design.
- Software development includes software design.
- Designers with many different skills are needed for complex products.

PROTOTYPES AND TESTING

Once a product has been designed, engineers build a test version of the product, called a prototype. A prototype shows any problems a designer might have overlooked. Designers make all the parts of the product, such as plastic cases, and source all the standard components, such as batteries and electronic components. They test all the parts individually, then they put the gadget together to test the complete gadget.

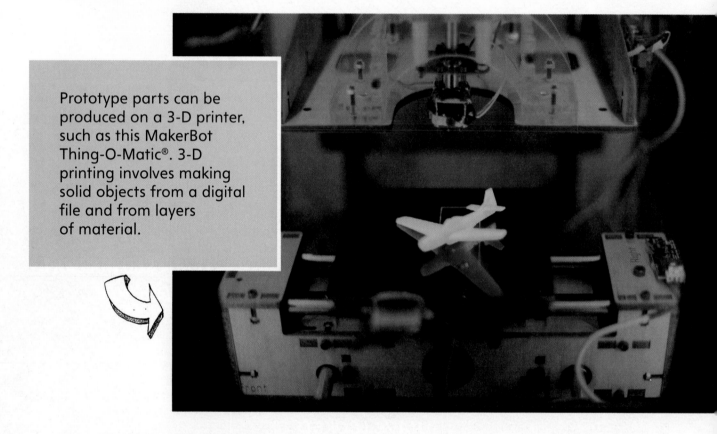

Prototype parts can be produced on a 3-D printer, such as this MakerBot Thing-O-Matic®. 3-D printing involves making solid objects from a digital file and from layers of material.

Prototype testing

All the systems of the prototype are tested. For example, on a tablet, battery life and communications such as Wi-Fi® are tested. Gadgets are also put through a series of physical tests. A cell phone might be dropped onto a solid surface hundreds of times to make sure it does not break. A power supply connector may be plugged into the gadget and removed again thousands of times to test the strength of the plug and socket.

Testing a gadget's software is a complex job, because there may be hundreds of different choices that a user could make when using the gadget, and all of these must be checked.

INTENSIVE TESTING

The JCB company makes tough phones for construction workers. Here are just some of the rigorous tests the phones go through:

- EVERY KEY ON THE KEYBOARD IS PRESSED 300,000 TIMES.

- EACH SIDE BUTTON ON THE CASE IS PRESSED 100,000 TIMES.

- A SIM CARD IS INSERTED AND REMOVED 3,000 TIMES.

- AN SD CARD IS INSERTED AND REMOVED 5,000 TIMES.

- CABLES ARE INSERTED AND PULLED OUT OF THE USB AND EARPHONE CONNECTORS 5,000 TIMES.

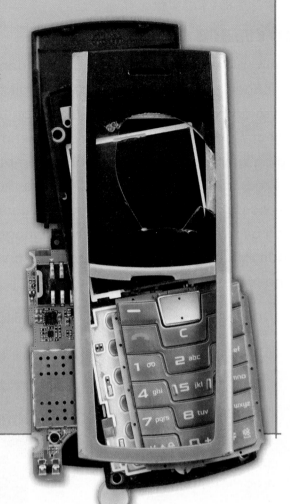

Prototype evaluation

A prototype gadget is checked to see if it meets the original requirements. If it does not, some parts or software may need to be redesigned and a new prototype needs to be built. Prototypes may also be given to groups of consumers to test and comment on. This process may be repeated many times before the prototype is finalized. Then, the gadget is ready to go into production.

THINK ABOUT IT

Can you estimate how many times you would press one of the buttons on a video game controller in a year? How often would you press it during a game? Multiply this number by the number of games you play each day, then multiply the answer by 365 to get your answer.

Software coding

System software for gadgets and video game consoles, game software for gadgets and consoles, and other application software must be written and tested before it is released on to the market. Writing software is called coding (and also sometimes software implementation or programming), and it is the job of computer programmers.

Programmers write software in code that a computer understands. The code is a list of instructions for the gadget's processor to carry out. It can be written in one of several languages. Examples of these are C and Java®. The language used depends on the gadget the software is going to be used on.

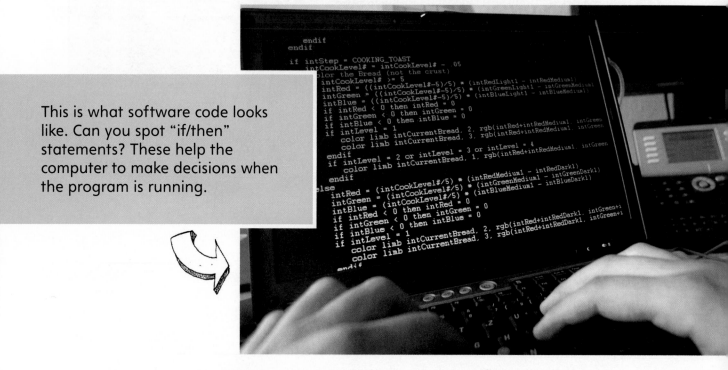

This is what software code looks like. Can you spot "if/then" statements? These help the computer to make decisions when the program is running.

Programmers write code that does the jobs software designers have decided are needed. A manufacturer might employ dozens or hundreds of programmers to write code, depending on the complexity of the gadget or game. Each programmer writes the code for one module of the software. Computers are sometimes used to write some code automatically, and some code is borrowed from software written for other systems.

Some programmers specialize in programming graphics or sound. Graphic programmers have to be expert mathematicians in order to produce realistic and fast-moving 3-D graphics.

LINES OF CODE

To create a big video console game, with 3-D graphics and dozens of levels and characters, programmers will have to write hundreds of thousands—sometimes millions—of lines of code. Operating systems are just as big. The **Android™** operating system for smartphones and tablets is made up of more than 12 million lines of code in different languages.

0101101010010011
0101101101010110
0101000101101010
1011010101101010
0100110101101100
1010110101010111
0110101011010100
0101101011011011

Software testing

Once software is written, it has to be tested. The software must be reliable and robust (which means it must not get off track and make the product stop working). Modules of code are tested individually before being combined to make the finished software. Any problems that are found during testing are called bugs. These can make the software give incorrect results, stop some features from working, or stop a gadget from working altogether.

Reprogramming to get rid of bugs is called debugging. Testing and debugging can take hundreds of hours. Some debugging is done by computer, using programs that automatically spot problems in the software. Bugs are even sometimes put in prototype software deliberately, to check the debugging process itself.

Testing and debugging software

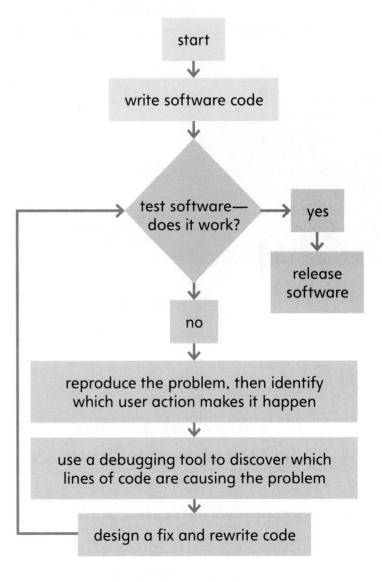

start

↓

write software code

↓

test software—does it work? → yes → release software

no

↓

reproduce the problem, then identify which user action makes it happen

↓

use a debugging tool to discover which lines of code are causing the problem

↓

design a fix and rewrite code

Patents

When manufacturers invent a new technology, they usually apply to the government for a **patent**. A patent office judges whether it really is a new invention. If it is, the office grants the patent to the manufacturer. This stops anybody from copying the invention. It means only a particular manufacturer has the right to make and sell a gadget that contains the new invention.

The idea of patents is to stop one company from stealing another's ideas. Companies can apply for patents for both software and hardware. There are often legal battles over patents. For example, in 2011, Apple and HTC argued over features of their touch-screen interfaces. However, companies often allow others to use their patents for a fee. Patents are also shared when gadgets need to use the same technologies to communicate (such as Bluetooth®).

Drawings form part of the patent application for devices that feature new ideas and technology.

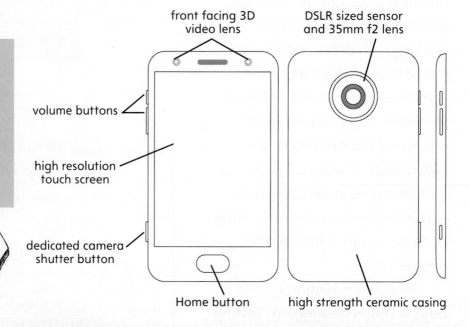

front facing 3D video lens

DSLR sized sensor and 35mm f2 lens

volume buttons

high resolution touch screen

dedicated camera shutter button

Home button

high strength ceramic casing

VIDEO GAME RATINGS

Video games must have an age rating on the packaging, and the rating must be displayed on a web site if the game is downloaded. The age rating shows what age of player the game is appropriate for. It helps stop children from playing games that have content (such as violence) that is not suitable for them. Game designers think about a player's age as they design a new game. In the United States, age ratings are awarded by the Entertainment Software Rating Board (ESRB).

Safety standards

All gadgets that are sold must be safe for people to use. This is very important—gadgets work with electricity and contain materials that could be toxic if they leak out. Manufacturers are responsible for making their products safe, especially since many users will be young children. In the United States and many other countries, electronic device manufacturers need to meet certain safety requirements before they can sell a product. Gadgets must also carry safety warnings where necessary. For example, gadget batteries must have a warning against taking them apart, because they contain hazardous chemicals.

This is a battery for a digital camera. As you can see, it carries warnings about its proper use and disposal.

WHAT HAVE WE LEARNED?

- A prototype is built to test that a product will work properly.
- A product may be redesigned if the prototype does not meet the original design requirements.
- Writing software is known as software coding.
- Software is debugged to remove errors.
- A patent protects new technology from being copied.
- Computer games have to carry an age rating.
- Gadgets must carry safety warnings.

PRODUCTION

Once a design specification is complete, thoughts can turn to production—which is where the gadget turns from an idea into reality. The first stage of production is to write a manufacturing specification for all the different components, from the complex integrated circuits to the screws that hold the case together. Some components, such as the plastic or metal case, will be specially made. Others, such as memory chips, will be existing parts that are sourced from other manufacturers.

Making tools

Before production can begin, tools must be made. These tools include molds for making plastic parts such as buttons. A factory must also be set up. This could be an existing factory or a completely new one that will need to be designed and built. Gadgets are frequently made in a different country from the one where the manufacturer is based, normally because labor costs there are lower. This is known as remote manufacturing.

Computer-aided manufacturing (CAM)

Lathes, milling machines, and drills are used to shape plastics and metals into components. These machine tools are controlled by CAM and automatically cut and drill away material. They are programmed with computer numerical control (CNC) and cut very accurately. Data from CAD files is fed to the machine tools, which make the components automatically. Designers think about how components will be manufactured as they design them, so that the components can be made easily and with as little waste as possible.

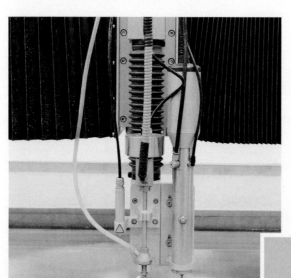

This is a numerically controlled cutting table. It is cutting components out of a sheet of steel.

Sourcing materials

The materials used to make the components for gadgets have to be sourced from somewhere. For example, aluminum, steel, gold, and silver are all used in gadgets. They are found in materials called ores, which are dug out of the ground in mines. The ores are processed to extract the metal—in the case of steel, iron is extracted and mixed with another element, usually carbon. The metal is then shaped into rods, bars, and sheets, ready for manufacturing. Most plastics are made from oil, which is also extracted from rock. Some gadget manufacturers make use of recycled plastics and metals, to reduce environmental damage.

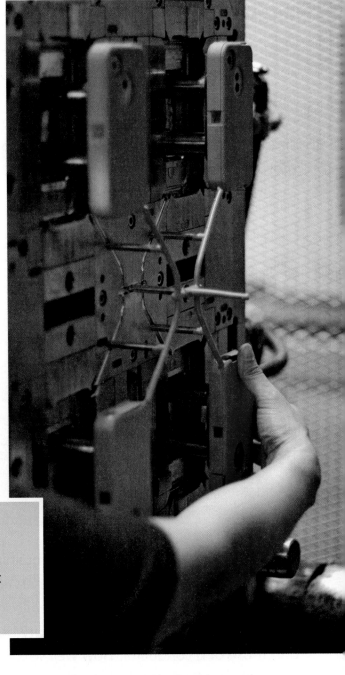

This is one part of a molding machine, from which brand new iPhone cases are being removed. The central section is where plastic is injected into the mold.

ECO IMPACT

Metals known as rare-earth metals are needed to manufacture many components of gadgets, including touch screens. They include tantalum and yttrium. The ores of these metals are hard to find. In 2011, 97 percent were mined in China. Toxic chemicals, including strong acids, are needed to process the ores, and in some places these have leaked out of processing plants, harming the environment. Some ores also contain radioactive materials, which are hard to dispose of.

Making integrated circuits

All gadgets need electronic circuits to make them work. Most are contained in integrated circuits, also known as silicon chips. An integrated circuit is made of silicon with microscopic electronic components built on its surface. Integrated circuits normally do a specific job. In a gadget or video game console, there will be one or more microprocessor chips, some memory chips, chips that produce graphics, and chips that produce sound.

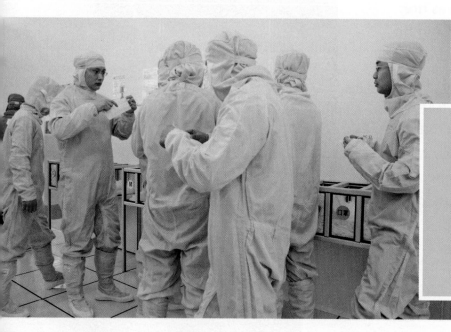

People who work in chip-manufacturing areas of gadget factories must wear special suits to keep the work space free of dust and dirt.

Dozens of integrated circuits are built in a grid pattern on a wafer of silicon up to 12 inches (30 centimeters) across and 1 millimeter thick. Silicon is used because it is a semiconductor—a material that has properties for conducting electricity between those of an insulator and those of a conductor. How well silicon conducts or insulates can be altered by adding other substances.

The components and connections are built up in layers on the wafer by a series of processes. Some processes add materials, such as metals, insulators, and semiconductors. Some change the electrical properties of the materials, and others remove materials from certain parts of the wafer. Specks of dust, high temperatures, and high humidity can ruin integrated circuits, so they are manufactured in a dust-free area called the factory's clean room. Here, temperature and humidity are carefully controlled.

Manufacturing an integrated circuit

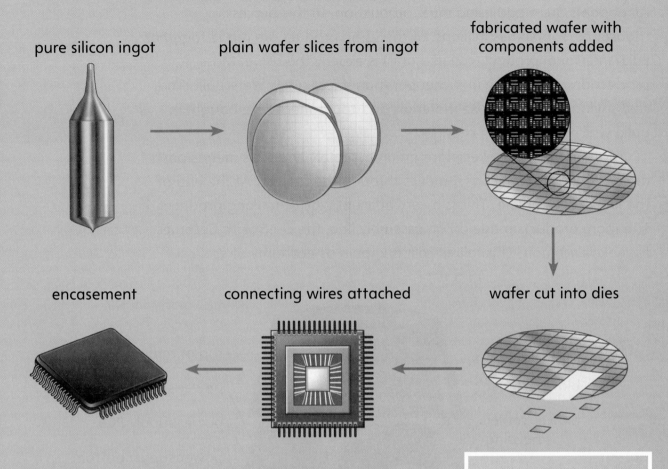

pure silicon ingot

plain wafer slices from ingot

fabricated wafer with components added

wafer cut into dies

connecting wires attached

encasement

This flow diagram shows the main steps involved in manufacturing a finished circuit from silicon.

HOW SMALL?

The tiny components on integrated circuits are measured in nanometers. How big is a nanometer?

- A millimeter equals a thousandth of a meter. (A meter is about 3.3 feet.)
- A micrometer equals a thousandth of a millimeter (or a millionth of a meter).
- A nanometer equals a thousandth of a micrometer (or a billionth of a meter).

A human hair is about 100,000 nanometers wide!

Mass production

All gadgets are made using mass production. In this process, thousands, sometimes millions, of the same product are made together. Each individual product (called a unit) is exactly the same. Mass production makes each unit cheaper than if just a few were built. The cost saving comes because materials and components are bought in bulk, which makes them cheaper.

Mass production takes place on an assembly line. This means parts are added to a product as it moves through the factory. At the end of the line, it is complete. This is a very efficient way of making products. The more products made on an assembly line, the cheaper it becomes to make each unit. This falling cost is known as economy of scale.

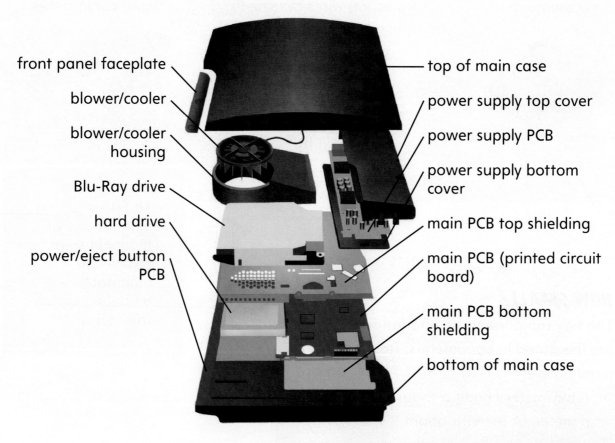

front panel faceplate

blower/cooler

blower/cooler housing

Blu-Ray drive

hard drive

power/eject button PCB

top of main case

power supply top cover

power supply PCB

power supply bottom cover

main PCB top shielding

main PCB (printed circuit board)

main PCB bottom shielding

bottom of main case

Here you can see all the parts of a Sony PlayStation that must be put together on an assembly line to create the finished product.

As a gadget moves along an assembly line, parts are added by workers and by robots. Each worker has a role on the assembly line, and many do skilled jobs, such as soldering electronic parts together. Robots are used to position parts accurately and quickly and may also do jobs such as soldering instead of workers. Workers make sure the assembly line is supplied with components. Some assembly lines run continuously, producing gadgets 24 hours a day.

QUALITY ASSURANCE AND CONTROL

Manufacturers operate a quality assurance system to ensure that the gadgets people buy are of high quality. When each item is complete, it is examined and tested by a quality control team. Automatic machines that test all the different features of the gadget at high speed may be used.

Assembly line workers must repeat the same task over and over again.

CONTRAST THE PAST

Mass production was developed hundreds of years ago, but automated assembly lines with robots were developed in the 1970s. Before then, all jobs on assembly lines were carried out by people, who could get tired and make mistakes. Robots and other automatic machines repeat tasks with the same accuracy and speed on every gadget that passes down the line. They have transformed manufacturing and improved the quality of products. However, people are still needed to make and maintain the robots and to carry out tasks that robots cannot do.

Software production

When software has been coded, it is just a computer file or collection of files, not a physical product. System software is loaded onto gadgets after they are produced. It is either loaded into a gadget's memory or onto its hard drive. Software that customers buy is either supplied on DVD or Blu-Ray discs, or it is downloaded from a manufacturer's web site.

Increasingly, software is downloaded rather than supplied on disc. Unlike discs, which need to be manufactured, no production is required for downloaded software. The computer files are simply copied from one computer to another.

On DVD and Blu-Ray discs, data is represented by microscopic pits in the disc surface. This is how a DVD is made:

- Molten plastic is forced into a mold containing a metal master disc.
- A plastic disc comes out of the mold with a pattern of pits on it.
- The plastic disc is coated with a thin layer of aluminum.
- A layer of protective plastic is added to the aluminum.
- A title is printed on the reverse side of the disc.

This is a DVD pressing machine in action. The process is completely automatic, and each DVD is exactly the same.

Product packaging

Packaging protects a gadget while it is transported from a factory to a store or to a customer, and while it is being stored. The packaging for a product also contains items such as a power supply, cables, and printed booklets. Packaging has to be designed and manufactured in time for gadgets to be packaged as they come off an assembly line. Packaging is made from paper, cardboard, and plastics.

BATCH PRODUCTION

DVDs and Blu-Ray discs are made by batch production. This means production is not continuous, as it is in mass production. A certain number of items are produced, then production stops and a different item is produced. For example, 10,000 DVDs of a game might be produced first, then 10,000 more when stores run out of stock.

Designers should try to use as little packaging as possible and use recyclable or biodegradable materials.

WHAT HAVE WE LEARNED?

- A manufacturing specification describes the parts of a gadget, what materials they are made from, and how they will be manufactured.
- In CAM, machine tools are controlled by computer, allowing them to make components very accurately.
- The metals and plastics used to make gadgets come from rocks or are made from oil.
- Gadgets are made by mass production on assembly lines.
- A quality assurance system ensures gadgets work properly when they leave the factory.

MARKETING

Marketing is about promoting and selling products. All gadget manufacturers have marketing departments that are responsible for making sure consumers know when new products are released and what advantages they offer.

Advertising

The main aim of advertising is to persuade people to part with their money and buy a new product. It is very important for manufacturers to sell as many units as possible, so they can make a profit and continue to produce goods. They often employ advertising agencies to run campaigns for them. Manufacturers or agencies will plan where and when to advertise. They will produce material for television, web sites, newspapers, and magazines. Advertisements are targeted at particular sections of the population, such as young people or wealthy professionals. It costs a lot of money to run a big advertising campaign, so a budget will have been set aside.

Advertisements are designed to show off the most desirable features of a product. These include how user-friendly it is, how much fun it is, its long battery life, the size of its screen, its speed, and its software, such as apps that allow access to social networks.

Despite the rise of Internet advertising, some manufacturers still believe printed ads are very effective. Here, a boy walks past a huge indoor ad in Seoul, Korea.

CONTRAST THE PAST

In the past, gadget manufacturers advertised in the print media, on television, and on billboards. In the 1990s, people began to connect to the Internet at home. This was the start of a revolution in marketing. Today, manufacturers advertise through their own web sites, through search engines, and with banner ads on related web sites. They also send e-mails to potential customers and maintain a presence on social-networking sites such as Facebook and Twitter.

SUCCESSFUL MARKETING

Amazon has sold millions of its Kindle e-book reader. Its clever advertising campaign emphasized the features that make the Kindle different from tablets, such as its low cost, e-ink screen, and lightness. Amazon also advertised the device on its own web site, which gets millions of hits a day.

You can scan an ad's quick response (QR) code with a smartphone. The code will connect the smartphone's browser to the product's web site.

Planning a campaign

Marketing begins with market research (see page 68). This takes place before a gadget is actually being manufactured. Advertisements need to be made and ready to appear just before the product becomes available to buy, so that consumers are aware of it and possibly looking out for it. Because most gadgets have a short life cycle, it is important there is no delay between a gadget first coming off the assembly line and sales being made. Otherwise, a rival manufacturer might capture the interest of the consumer and make a sale instead.

Product launch

When a gadget or game is ready to sell, its manufacturer organizes a product launch. This is an effective way to raise awareness of a new product and to create a sense of excitement around it. In the lead-up to the launch, newspaper and television ads will appear and a web site will go live.

Manufacturers may also organize a launch event, where the new gadget or game is shown off to experts and the media. They can try it out and write reviews of it, which also helps to raise consumer interest. A good product launch will create a high demand for the product when it is released.

This enormous crowd is waiting for the launch of the latest Apple iPhone.

FAIL

Not all gadgets are a success. In 2006 Microsoft launched the first of its Zune® range of portable media players to compete with Apple's iPod. Although many reviewers said the Zune was a good product, especially some of the software, it did not have enough marketing support to compete with the established iPod. The Zune players were withdrawn in 2011.

Gadget and video game fans eagerly wait for the launch of a new product. It is important that there are enough units of a gadget or game available when it is launched, because otherwise demand may outstrip supply. This means supplies will run out and consumers will have to wait before they can buy—with the possibility they will turn to a competitor's product instead.

Sales figures measure how many units are bought each week, month, or year. When first released, the figures begin to rise. They will usually rise for a few months, then they stop rising during the maturity phase. They will then begin to fall until the product is no longer available, when they hit zero. This rise and fall in sales is part of a product's life cycle.

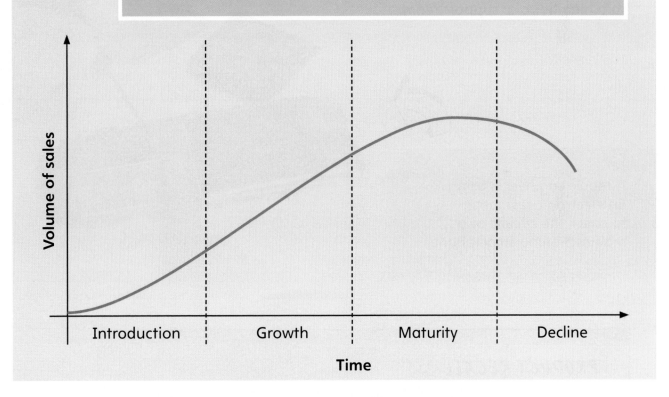

WHAT HAVE WE LEARNED?
- Marketing is about advertising and selling products.
- Successful marketing encourages consumer interest.
- A product launch can create high demand.

PRODUCT MAINTENANCE

A company's involvement in a product's life cycle does not end on the day the product is sold. Product maintenance comes next. This means keeping a product working while it is being used—this stage is called its useful life. Like all other products, gadgets should be made to a good standard. They should be reliable, which means they should work for a reasonable length of time without malfunctioning or breaking. By law, manufacturers have to guarantee their gadgets for a certain amount of time (normally a year). This is written in a product's warranty.

Manufacturers also provide support for their customers, to help those who are having problems making their gadgets work properly. Online support is provided on a manufacturer's web site. There will be a list of common questions, known as frequently asked questions (FAQs). Customers may also be able to talk to a member of a support team.

A repair engineer is using an electronic test meter to check the circuits of a malfunctioning smartphone.

PRODUCT RECALL

Occasionally, a product might not work properly or may develop a problem that makes it unsafe to use. In these cases, the product is recalled. This means customers can send their gadgets back to the manufacturer to be repaired or replaced.

Spares and repairs

Manufacturers make spare parts for their gadgets, which are used to replace parts that may get damaged or broken accidentally. Because gadgets have a short life cycle, their parts are rarely used long enough to wear out. Normally, the only part that might have to be replaced in a gadget is the battery, which can lose its ability to hold a charge after being recharged a few thousand times. If a gadget does develop a problem, it can usually be repaired by the manufacturer.

All batteries are marked with a recycling symbol to remind people to take them to a recycling center like this one after they are used up.

ECO IMPACT

Batteries contain many toxic chemicals, including metals such as lead, cadmium, nickel, and lithium. If batteries are thrown into landfill sites, these chemicals can leak into the soil and into water in the ground, with possible damage to plants and animals. So, when batteries in gadgets are replaced, the old batteries should be taken to a recycling center. Then, some of the materials can be extracted and used again.

Software updates

Gadgets and video game consoles could not work without their software. Software does not break down the way physical parts can, but it can have irritating bugs in it that are not spotted at the software testing stage of the life cycle. These are often spotted by users and reported to the manufacturer. Sometimes different applications can stop each other from working properly.

Reasons for software updates

Bugs mean that software sometimes needs to be rewritten slightly to make it work properly. This is called a software update. Sometimes the update is just a small piece of code, called a patch. At other times, the software is completely replaced with a new version. An update is shown in the software version number (for example, version 2.1 becomes version 2.2). New versions of software normally solve several bugs all at once and may add new features. Software updates lengthen the life cycle of a gadget, because they improve the gadget with a simple operation.

AUTOMATIC UPDATES

Software updates often happen automatically. A gadget checks the manufacturer's web site every few days to make sure its software is up-to-date. If an update is available, the gadget downloads it, after checking with the user. Minor software updates are free, as they are needed to keep a gadget working properly. Major updates normally have to be paid for.

Malware

Malware—such as viruses, worms, and trojan horses—is software that damages a computer or stops it from working properly. Viruses and worms spread in e-mails or over computer networks. Trojan horses do not spread, but they get into a computer unnoticed by the user and do damage.

Gadgets such as smartphones and tablets are really computers, and so people are writing malware for them. Malware is a problem for gadget users and costs time and money to get rid of. To avoid malware, always be careful which apps you download and think about installing anti-virus software.

How malware is spread

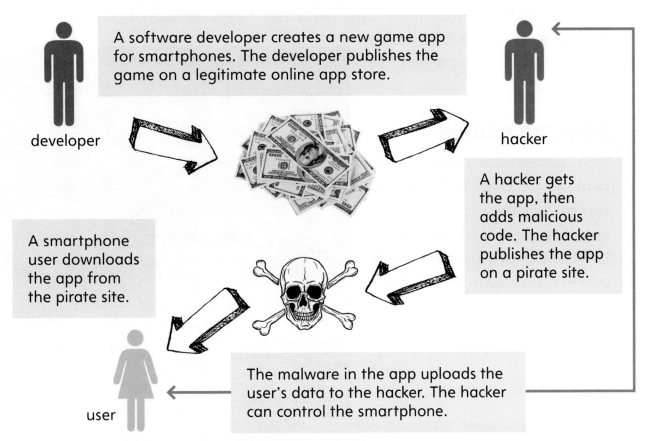

developer

A software developer creates a new game app for smartphones. The developer publishes the game on a legitimate online app store.

hacker

A hacker gets the app, then adds malicious code. The hacker publishes the app on a pirate site.

A smartphone user downloads the app from the pirate site.

The malware in the app uploads the user's data to the hacker. The hacker can control the smartphone.

user

WHAT HAVE WE LEARNED?
- Product maintenance keeps a gadget working after it has been sold.
- Manufacturers produce spare parts for mending their products.
- Software updates fix minor bugs in software.

END OF LIFE

A gadget's life cycle comes to an end when it is no longer used. Consumers stop using millions of gadgets every year. They become electronic waste (e-waste). So, what happens to them?

Some are thrown away, and so come to the end of their lives. Others end up sitting in a drawer until they become obsolete. This is a waste—the life cycles of gadgets can be extended by re-using them. When a gadget does reach the end of its life—either obsolete, worn out, or broken—its components and materials can be recycled.

Reusing gadgets

A gadget can be reused by passing it on to a family member or friend. There are also many charities that refurbish old gadgets. Refurbishment means getting a gadget ready to be sold to a new user. In the case of a cell phone, for example, the charity checks that the phone has not been stolen, repairs it if necessary, cleans and repackages it, and then sells it.

Reusing games

Video games have a different end to their cycle. Downloaded games stay on computers or devices until they are deleted. Games on DVDs or Blu-ray discs are normally passed on or sold to other users, sometimes many times. They have life cycles that last many years.

Old cell phones can be sent to countries where there are few landlines and where many people cannot afford the latest gadgets.

REFURBISHMENT

In addition to charities, some gadget manufacturers will refurbish old cell phones, too. Some cell phones are known as "beyond economic repair," meaning they cannot usefully be reused. However, about 95 percent can be refurbished. If you do pass on a cell phone in this way, remember to delete as much personal data as possible before you do.

ECO IMPACT

If a gadget is simply thrown away at the end of its life, the energy and materials used to make it are lost, which is bad for the environment. Here are some eco-friendly options that manufacturers and users can choose:

End of life

Reuse: Pass gadgets on to new users.

Recycle: Get back materials and use them in new products.

Refuse: Don't buy gadgets that you don't need or that use lots of packaging.

Reduce: Cut down on the amount of materials used and keep gadgets for longer before replacing them.

Rethink: Redesign gadgets to use less energy.

Recycling

When a gadget is recycled, it is broken down into its components. The materials in the components are extracted and become raw materials for new products. Gadget design should make it easy for the device to be broken up at the end of its life. In most cases, about 80 percent of the materials in a gadget can be recycled. The phone manufacturer Nokia claims that 100 percent of the materials in its phones are recyclable.

The materials we can recover from gadgets are mostly plastics and metals. Touch screens and integrated circuits use metals that are rare and hard to find in rocks. This means recycling them is very important.

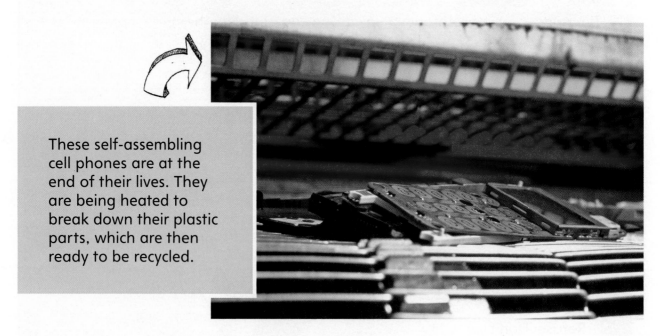

These self-assembling cell phones are at the end of their lives. They are being heated to break down their plastic parts, which are then ready to be recycled.

Recycling methods

You cannot sort the parts of a gadget into different materials yourself, as you do with the recyclable materials in household waste. You should take gadgets to your local recycling center. Specialized recycling companies carry out the recycling process.

We have finally reached the end of the life cycle of a gadget. However, the materials used to make it may live on in new products. Its components, including electrical connectors, screens, keyboards, camera lenses, and speakers, may be used again, too. Cardboard and paper from gadget packaging can be recycled. These materials and components enter a new life cycle.

LANDFILL

Unfortunately, many people are unaware that gadgets can and should be recycled. Millions of old and broken gadgets still end up in landfill, wasting the energy and materials used to make them. The gadgets will take thousands of years to break down and will then leave potentially hazardous chemicals in the ground. This is the worst thing that can happen to a gadget at the end of its life.

This is the WEEE (waste electrical and electronic equipment) Man—a 23-foot (7-meter), 3.3-ton sculpture at the Eden Project in Cornwall, England. It represents the amount of this kind of waste the average British household throws away in a lifetime.

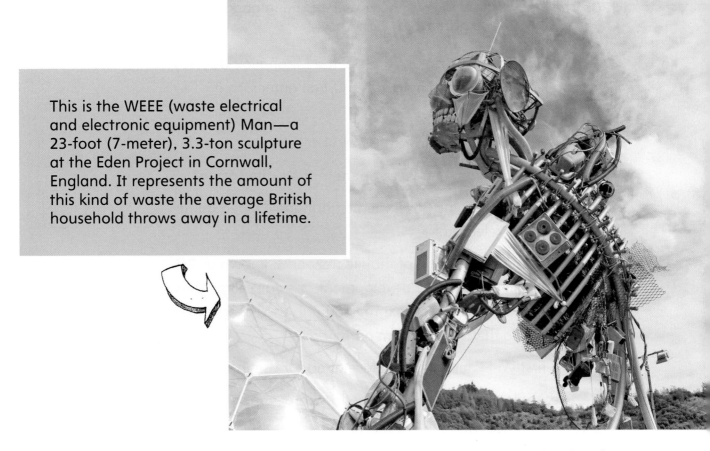

WHAT HAVE WE LEARNED?

- End of life is when a gadget is obsolete or broken beyond repair.
- Reusing or refurbishing a gadget extends its life cycle.
- Most of the materials in a gadget can be recycled.
- Many gadgets still end up in landfill sites.

TIMELINE

1913 The Ford Motor Company perfects a moving assembly line for the production of the Ford Model T™ car.

1958 The integrated circuit is invented.

1958 Hard-wearing plastic called polycarbonate is invented.

1961 The first industrial robot, a UNIMATE, starts work in the General Motors car factory in Ewing Township, New Jersey.

1963 The first CAD system is developed.

1970s Light-emitting diodes (LEDs) are first used in gadgets for displays and indication lights.

1972 The first electronic game console, the Magnavox Odyssey, is released. It plays simple bat-and-ball games on a television screen.

1974 The first transparent touch screen is developed.

1978 The first cell phone network opens in the United States.

1989 The Nintendo Game Boy®, the first handheld video game console, is released.

1990s The second generation of mobile networks, known as **2G**, opens, allowing for the development of small cell phones and the introduction of text messaging. Also, people begin to connect to the Internet from home.

1991 The first Wi-Fi networks are developed for use in stores.

1993 The Apple company releases the Newton®, a personal digital assistant (PDA) with a touch screen.

1994 The Entertainment Software Rating Board (ESRB) is formed to ensure that the content of video games is appropriate for different audiences.

1994 The first generation Sony PlayStation video game console is released.

1996 The digital versatile disc (DVD) is introduced.

1998 The first MP3 music players are released.

1998 The driving game Gran Turismo for the PlayStation is released.

2000s The third generation **(3G)** mobile networks open, allowing mobile devices to download data.

2001 The first generation Microsoft Xbox is launched.

2001 Apple begins to sell its first MP3 player, the iPod.

2002 The BlackBerry is one of the first smartphones available to buy.

2004 The first Nintendo DS® handheld console is released, as is the PlayStation Portable® (PSP).

2005 The Xbox 360® is released.

2006 The Nintendo Wii console is released, with its revolutionary motion control system.

2006 The PlayStation 3® is released.

2007 The first Apple iPhone is released.

2007 The Kindle is released by Amazon.

2007 The Android operating system is released for mobile devices.

2010 The Xbox Kinect® is launched, allowing players to control games with body movement.

2010 The first Apple iPad is released.

2010 The Ninento 3DS® is the first portable console with a 3-D screen.

GLOSSARY

2G, 3G, and **4G** generations of mobile data networks, which have allowed mobile devices to have increasing speeds of communication and features (such as text messaging, media messaging, and web browsing)

Android operating system used on many smartphones and tablets

application (app) software that makes a gadget do a specific job

assembly line system of mass production in which products are assembled from their components as they move along a conveyor belt

cloud computing system in which data and applications are delivered to devices via the Internet, rather than being stored on the device itself

component part of something bigger

computer-aided design (CAD) use of computer technology for the process of designing objects

computer-aided manufacturing (CAM) use of information and computer technology in the manufacturing of products, normally in conjunction with CAD

constraint limitation on how something is made

design process of choosing the materials, components, and appearance of a gadget

engineering use of mathematics and science to design and build structures, machines, devices, systems, and processes

input information that goes into a system

integrated circuit electronic circuit made up of microscopic components built into a slice of silicon

manufacturing process of actually making products from materials and components

marketing bringing a gadget or game to the attention of the consumer; to try to sell the gadget

mass production process of manufacturing identical products in large numbers

operating system software that controls the parts of a gadget itself. Examples include Apple's iOS and Google's Android.

output information that comes out of a system

patent authority from a government that allows a manufacturer sole right to make a product or component

process what happens to information between the input and output of a system

product life cycle series of events in the life of a gadget, from initial idea through to design, manufacturing, useful life, and disposal or recycling

prototype one of the first examples of a product to be made, so that it can be tested to make sure it works properly

recycling processing old materials and products to make new materials and products. Recycling saves raw materials and reduces waste.

requirements in design, necessities affecting the cost or function of a final product or service

smartphone cell phone, normally with a color touch screen, that allows voice calls, texting, e-mailing, and web browsing and runs other applications

software instructions and data that control what a gadget or video game console does

software design figuring out how software for gadgets and games will work

specification list of requirements and constraints for a product

system set of things that work together to do a job. All systems have an input, a process, and an output.

technology modifying objects and materials to satisfy people's needs and wants

useful life part of the life cycle of a product when the product is being used

Screen Time Can Mess with the Body's "Clock"

Reading on an iPad® in the evening can make it hard for the body to fall asleep

by Andrew Bridges

Reprinted from SocietyForScience.org, February 9, 2015

For a good night's sleep, here is some expert advice: Turn off, turn in and drop off.

Anyone who does the opposite—say, turning on an iPad or other similar electronic reader in bed—may have a harder time both dropping off to sleep and shaking that groggy feeling the next morning. That's the conclusion of a new study.

Sleep experts at Brigham and Women's Hospital in Boston, Massachusetts, found that the light from a tablet computer upsets the body's internal clock. And that can create real health and safety risks, the researchers say. Reading a printed book did not have the same effect. They reported their findings January 27 in the *Proceedings of the National Academy of Sciences.*

An internal "clock" helps regulate when we eat, sleep and wake. Exposure to the light of day and darkness of night keeps its timing set to a roughly 24-hour cycle.

For instance, starting about two hours before bedtime, our brains start to produce a hormone called melatonin. It signals our internal clock that darkness has fallen. It also prepares the body for sleep.

Scientists long have known that light at night can disrupt that internal clock. And it does so by suppressing melatonin. This prevents the body from getting the message that bedtime is near.

Electronic devices with lit screens are now hugely popular. They have added another source of artificial light at night. The new study looked specifically at the iPad. Apple has sold more than 225 million of these tablets since their introduction in 2010.

For their new study, the researchers recruited six men and six women, all in their mid 20s. Over two weeks, each spent four hours reading each evening before a 10 P.M. bedtime. The volunteers read on an iPad for five nights in a row. On another five consecutive evenings they read a printed book.

The researchers noted how long it took the volunteers to fall asleep, how long they spent asleep and how long they remained in each stage of sleep. The experts also took blood samples to measure melatonin levels.

People took nearly 10 minutes longer to fall asleep, on average, after reading on the iPads. They also spent less time in rapid-eye movement (or REM) sleep. This sleep phase appears important for learning and storing memories.

There was no difference in hours spent sleeping after reading from either the iPad or a printed book. But how volunteers felt the next day did differ.

"Our most surprising finding was that individuals using the e-reader would be more tired and take longer to become alert the next morning," says sleep researcher Anne-Marie Chang.

The tablet computer has become a part of the lives of hundreds of millions of people, young and old. A new study finds reading on them before bedtime can hurt our sleep.

"This has real consequences for daytime functioning," she says. "And these effects might be worse in the real world as opposed to the controlled environment we used." A co-author of the study, she works at Pennsylvania State University in University Park. Previously, she worked at Brigham and Women's Hospital.

Lighting scientist Mariana Figueiro calls the study thorough. She also finds its results unsurprising. Figueiro, who was not connected to this new study, works at Rensselaer Polytechnic Institute in Troy, N.Y. Her research has shown that spending even two hours on an iPad before bedtime can cut down the brain's release of melatonin.

While she generally liked the study, she was concerned about "its applicability to real life." This experiment was done in a laboratory setting under very dim lights. And that, she says, may not mimic how most people use e-readers—or read printed books.

"It's not necessarily true," she says, "that books are okay but e-readers are not." She notes that "If you turn on a very bright light to read, it may have the same effect."

What's more, she points out, spending plenty of time exposed to natural light during the day can reduce the body's sensitivity to artificial light at night. "The same iPad may have a much stronger effect on kids who stay *indoors* during the day, in dim light," Figueiro says, "than on kids who play outdoors."

Regularly getting too little sleep can pose important health risks. For instance, studies have shown that it can up the risk of everything from obesity, diabetes and depression to car accidents.

POWER WORDS

body clock (also known as biological clock) A mechanism present in all life forms that controls when various functions such as metabolic signals, sleep cycles or photosynthesis should occur.

circadian rhythm Biological functions such as body temperature and sleeping/waking times that operate on a roughly 24-hour cycle.

hormone A chemical produced in a gland and then carried in the bloodstream to another part of the body. Hormones control many important body activities, such as growth. Hormones act by triggering or regulating chemical reactions in the body.

melatonin A hormone secreted in the evening by a structure in the brain. Melatonin tells the body that it is nearing time to sleep. It plays a key role in regulating circadian rhythms.

REM sleep A period of sleep that takes its name for the rapid eye movement, or REM, that occurs. People dream during REM sleep, but their bodies can't move. In non-REM sleep, breathing and brain activity slow, but people can still move about.

tablet (in computing) A small, hand-held computer that can connect to the Internet and that users can control using a touch screen. An Apple iPad, Samsung Galaxy® and Amazon Kindle Fire® are all examples of tablets.

obesity (Condition of being) extremely overweight. Obesity is associated with a wide range of health problems, including type 2 diabetes and high blood pressure.

A Bright Idea

written by
Susan Ring

Contents

Life Before the Light Bulb

Suppose that it's the middle of the night and you are staying at a relative's house. You need to get a glass of water, but the house is dark and unfamiliar. What would you do? Most likely you would turn on a light to find the kitchen or bathroom. After getting yourself a drink, you would switch off the lights as you returned to bed.

Now suppose what life would be like if you could not easily turn lights on and off as you needed them. You might have to rely on the Sun and the Moon as your main sources of light. That's what it was like for people thousands of years ago. Light bulbs and electricity did not exist. Although early people had probably discovered fire, they had to learn how to control it to provide light when and where it was needed.

Over thousands of years, people developed different light sources that led to the electric lights we have today. This is the story of those developments and how they changed human life and civilization.

Fire was the first light source people were able to control. Scientists believe that this happened around 100,000 years ago. Most likely, a person first lit a branch or stick from a natural source, such as a smoldering tree that had been struck by lightning, and then learned to maintain the flame. Fire then provided people with a consistent light source. It also gave them warmth. Because animals were often afraid of fire, it kept early humans safer as well.

The ability to control fire was probably the first step toward human civilization. By spending time together around the fire, people built a sense of community. Extended hours of light may also have helped people to make better tools, plan for hunts, and cook foods.

A campfire kept early people warm, provided safety from wild animals, and lengthened working hours by providing light.

First Light Sources

The first fires were probably located in one spot or hearth, around which people gathered. However, evidence shows that early people soon discovered how to carry fire with them. They made torches from sticks or reeds dipped in animal fat. Although these torches provided a handy light source, the open flames could be dangerous. In addition, a torch large enough to provide light for any length of time was probably heavy and hard to handle.

Then, about 70,000 years ago, people began to make the first lamps. They used hard stone pounding tools to form hollow areas in softer stones, collected shells, or shaped and dried clay. Then they poured animal fat into the hollow and added moss or straw. The moss or straw absorbed the fat and held the flame. This is similar to how a wick, the string in a candle or an oil lamp, absorbs the wax or oil that keeps a flame burning.

Stones were hollowed out to make crude lamps.

A shell could be used as a lamp by adding oil and a wick.

Pottery oil lamps were used in ancient Rome.

Candles

Between 3000 B.C. and 2000 B.C., people in Egypt made torches called rushlights by soaking the core of reeds in animal fat. Although rushlights were the predecessors of candles, they did not have true wicks, which allow candles to burn longer. The Romans were the first to weave fibers together and use them as candle wicks. In fact, the word *candle* comes from *candere*, a Latin word meaning "to shine."

Ancient candles and lamps primarily used tallow—animal fat—for fuel, but tallow gave off a strong smell when it burned. By the fourth century A.D., people in China began making candles from beeswax, the substance secreted by honeybees to make honeycombs. Beeswax was a much better fuel than tallow because it smelled better and was not as smoky. Beeswax candles were very expensive, though, so only wealthy people could afford them. In the late eighteenth century, candles made from spermaceti, or whale oil, were introduced. These candles were not as expensive as beeswax candles, so more people could afford to use them.

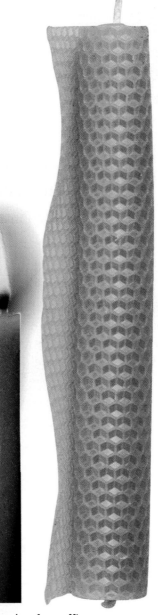

Today, most candles are made of paraffin wax (left). Beeswax (right) is also used.

The Search for a Better Light

During the late eighteenth and early nineteenth centuries, some new and cheaper sources of lighting were developed. Fossil fuels, such as petroleum and coal, found deep in the earth, became especially popular.

In 1792, Scottish engineer William Murdock began experimenting with coal gas, which was produced by heating coal. At first, he used the gas to light lanterns around his home and his company's factory. By 1804, Murdock had placed 900 gaslights in cotton mills and had become known as the father of the gas industry.

In 1821, natural gas began to gain popularity. It worked much like coal gas, but natural gas forms inside the earth and does not need to be manufactured. One of the first places to use natural gas was Fredonia, New York. Natural gas from a 27-foot-deep well was piped to buildings and used for light. Some places, however, did not have natural gas deposits and so could not take advantage of this fuel.

early gas lamp

Gas lighting changed the look of London, England, and many other cities.

Early Experiments in Electricity

Electricity is found in many forms. It appears in the sky as powerful lightning bolts. It darts through the human body as nerve impulses. Electric pulses are also used by animals such as the electric ray to stun prey.

As far back as the fifth and sixth centuries B.C., people tried to understand the nature of electricity. In 600 B.C., Thales, a Greek mathematician, became curious about what is now known as static electricity. Thales rubbed wool over a piece of amber (a yellowish substance usually made of fossilized tree resin or sap). He discovered that once amber had been rubbed, it acquired static electricity and could attract lightweight objects such as straw, feathers, and hair.

When rubbed, amber acquires static electricity and can attract lightweight objects. The Greek word for *amber* is *elektron*, which is the origin of the word *electricity*.

Electric rays use electric pulses to stun their prey.

Electricity: Static vs. Current
Static electricity consists of charges that do not flow. When a person or thing comes into contact with an object holding static electricity, there is a discharge, causing a shock. On the other hand, current electricity flows through wires. It can be generated in a battery or by a generator powered by steam, oil, or other fuels. It can then be sent to power such items as radios, televisions, and computers.

Collecting Electrical Charges

The Leyden jar, first used in the Netherlands in 1746, was developed by early experimenters to store electric charges.

In the mid-1700s, Dutch scientists worked on ways to collect and store energy. They invented the Leyden jar, which was a glass container with metal foil on the inside and outside. The top of the jar was placed against a machine that generated static electricity, which was then collected in the jar. The static electricity remained in the jar until a wire (or anything that conducts electricity) touched the inside and outside foil—which caused the electricity to discharge, creating sparks.

In 1747, American scientist and inventor Benjamin Franklin experimented with electricity. Franklin noticed the similarities between the Leyden jar's tiny sparks and the giant sparks made by lightning. He thought they might both be forms of electricity, even though they were different in power and size.

Franklin's experiments with electricity also led to his invention of the lightning rod in 1752. This metal rod attracts static electricity from a storm cloud. Because it draws lightning and is placed higher than other buildings around it, it protects buildings and people from being struck by lightning.

A lightning rod draws the charge from a storm cloud and conducts it into the ground, thus protecting buildings from taking the charge and possibly catching fire.

The First Battery

Italian scientist Count Alessandro Volta was also curious about the mysterious properties of electricity. He wanted to store an electric charge, but he also wanted to produce a steady flow of electricity. The Leyden jar could only give off short bursts of electric sparks.

Count Alessandro Volta

In 1800, Volta invented the Voltaic Pile. This device, made of copper and zinc disks, had pasteboard soaked in salt water in between the disks. Volta stacked the disks about 12 inches high. At the bottom of the stack was a copper disk—the positive terminal of the pile. At the top was a zinc disk—the negative terminal. The stack was held together by three glass rods. Volta showed that a low current of electricity flowed from the device when a wire was attached to either end. He had made the first chemical battery and, for the first time, showed how to produce a continuous electric current.

Voltaic Pile

zinc

pasteboard

copper

How a Battery Works

Volta showed that stacking two different metals, each separated only by a moist, porous material, causes a chemical reaction that generates electricity. Today, batteries are made with many combinations of elements. Like Volta's pile, however, they all have negative and positive terminals. The unit of electric potential is the volt, named after the Count.

An Arc of Light

Humphry Davy, an English chemist, invented the first electric light. In 1809, he connected one wire to the negative terminal of a huge Voltaic Pile and another wire to the positive terminal. Then, between the other ends of the wires he placed a charcoal strip. (Charcoal is made mostly of carbon and is created by burning wood or other material.) The charcoal glowed, demonstrating that battery (electric) power could be used to produce light. He also passed an electric current through many other materials. When he passed it through a platinum wire, the wire glowed.

Through his many experiments, Davy discovered that if he ran an electric current through two charcoal rods placed slightly apart, a curved band of electric current jumped from one rod to the other. This discovery, called an electric arc, eventually led to arc lamps, which were first used in a lighthouse in 1862. They gave off a very bright, white light.

Humphry Davy discovered the electric arc.

This arc lamp dates from the 1870s.

The Light Bulb Is Born

Warren de la Rue

In 1820, British scientist Warren de la Rue placed a platinum coil in an airless glass tube. He knew that platinum had a very high melting point and believed that it would not melt when an electric current was passed through it. He also thought that if he removed the air from the tube, or created a vacuum, the platinum would not catch fire. Air, after all, is needed for burning. The scientist had made the first incandescent light bulb, which means its light was made by heating a material until it glowed. Unfortunately, platinum was too expensive for de la Rue's light bulb to be of any practical use.

About 20 years later, an Englishman named Frederick de Moleyns also created a light bulb, which he patented. His light bulb also used an airless glass tube, but de Moleyns placed powdered charcoal between two platinum wires. One problem with de Moleyns' bulb was that the charcoal completely blackened the glass as it burned, quickly dimming the light.

What Are Patents?

A patent is a legal protection granted by the government to safeguard a citizen's ideas and inventions. If someone copies a patented invention without permission, the inventor may sue or take other legal action. Patents allow people to share their ideas and inventions with society free from the fear that others might steal them and unjustly make money from them.

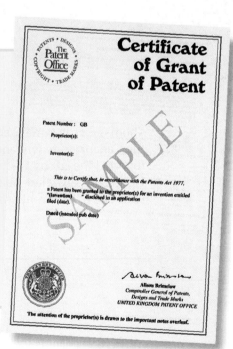

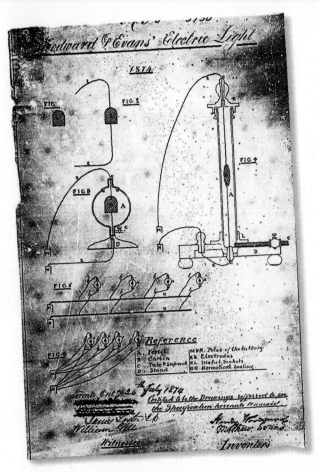

Woodward's and Evans' patent included detailed drawings of their invention.

In 1874, Henry Woodward and Matthew Evans of Canada filed a Canadian patent for their version of the incandescent bulb. In 1876, they obtained a U.S. patent on what they now called the electric lamp. To create light, the Canadian team used a threadlike piece of carbon that would glow when an electric current was passed through it. Their glass bulb was filled with nitrogen gas to prevent the carbon strip from burning up.

Unfortunately, Woodward and Evans did not have enough money to perfect their invention. In 1879, American inventor Thomas Edison, who had developed similar ideas, purchased the U.S. patent from the inventors. With the support of wealthy investors, such as the Vanderbilts and J. P. Morgan, Edison began the Edison Electric Light Company to further develop his ideas.

Thomas Edison purchased the Canadians' patent and founded the Edison Electric Light Company. Here he sits with one of his inventions.

The Modern Light Bulb

Joseph Swan demonstrated his light bulb in England in 1878.

Although Thomas Edison is often credited with inventing the light bulb, British scientist Joseph Swan also patented a version of the incandescent light bulb. He received his patent in 1878—ten months before Edison received his. Swan had begun work on his bulb in 1860. It featured an almost airless tube and a carbon fiber filament. Though his bulb worked, it had a short lifespan, and the light it produced was very dim. These weaknesses were caused by several problems. First, the vacuum pumps Swan used did not remove enough air from the bulb. The presence of oxygen caused the filament to burn up quickly. Second, the material the filament was made from required a great deal of electric current to run through it before it became hot and glowed. Finally, Swan's power source was a battery, which was not strong enough to produce a bright light.

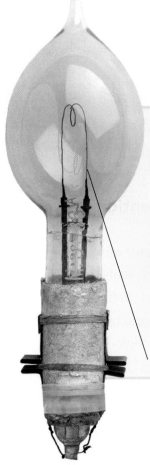

What Is a Filament?

The material that glows in the center of a light bulb is called a filament. Early light bulbs had carbon filaments. Today, filaments are made from the metal tungsten, which was discovered in 1783. Edison considered using tungsten as a filament in the 1880s, but the brittle metal was hard to work with.

Swan's bulb had a carbon filament.

Most modern bulbs have tungsten filaments.

Edison's Menlo Park research team

Edison Improves the Light Bulb

In the same year that Joseph Swan patented his light bulb, Edison told a *New York Sun* newspaper reporter that he was sure that he could create a light that everybody would use. Even though several kinds of incandescent bulbs had been invented, most homes and streets were still lit by gas because none of the bulbs worked very well. All the previous work on light bulbs, however, gave Edison clues about the approaches his research team should and should not take.

Edison's Invention Factory

Edison's laboratory was stocked with many books, tools, and chemicals. About an hour away from the hustle and bustle of New York City, Menlo Park provided a perfect environment for creative thinking.

The Menlo Park Team

Edison assembled a team of experts to assist him in his laboratory in Menlo Park, New Jersey. From 1878 to 1880, the scientists worked tirelessly to perfect an incandescent light bulb. The hardest part of their job was determining which material worked best as a filament. Edison knew that anything with carbon would eventually burn up, but he wanted to find the substance that would glow the longest.

The Menlo Park team tried thousands of fibers—everything from human hair to fishing line to spider webs. Edison even had samples of vegetable and plant fibers sent to him from around the world. Each fiber had to be made as thin as thread and baked until it was black with carbon. Edison experimented with thousands of materials—more than 6,000 plants alone—to determine which would let the bulb glow for an extended period of time.

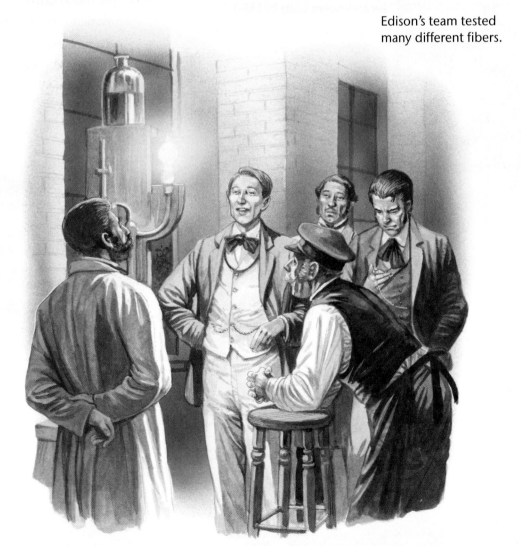

Edison's team tested many different fibers.

On the Right Track

Edison kept the team working day and night on delicate, painstaking experiments. Finally, in October 1879, they tried a carbonized cotton thread filament that glowed for nearly 15 hours. Edison knew that he was at last on the right track. No other material had glowed nearly as long.

By the end of 1880, Edison and his Menlo Park team had produced a bulb that burned for more than 200 hours! They used Japanese bamboo in a strong vacuum to produce such a long-lasting bulb. The team was well on its way to developing the modern light bulb.

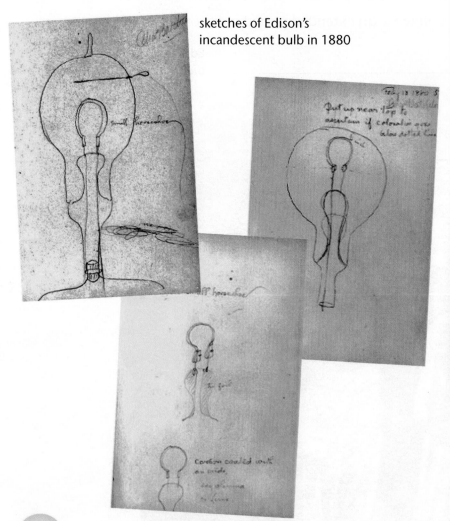

sketches of Edison's incandescent bulb in 1880

Becoming an Inventor

By the time he was 22, Thomas Edison had set up his invention factory and was determined to produce a new invention every ten days. He succeeded. Edison applied for a patent each week and created a major new invention every six months. The phonograph (shown below)—an early form of record player—earned him the nickname of the Wizard of Menlo Park. Of course, his best-known invention was the affordable, long-lasting light bulb.

Perfecting the Pump

Finding a good filament was not the team's only challenge. Many glass bulbs were needed for experiments, so Edison had to hire glassblowers. A filament then had to be carefully inserted into each bulb before the air could be removed and the base sealed.

Although Swan had developed a good vacuum pump in 1878, the pump still left a small amount of air in the bulbs. Edison realized that any air would speed up destruction of the filament. As a result, his research team made important improvements to Swan's pump. Eventually they were able to create a very strong vacuum in each bulb.

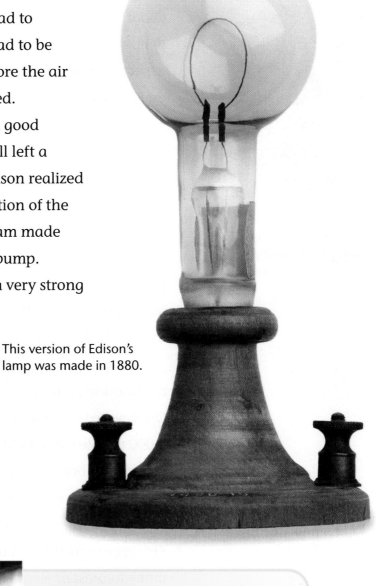

This version of Edison's lamp was made in 1880.

Glassblowing

In the late 1800s, glass was still being made by hand. The glassblower blew air into a hollow metal rod with a glob of red-hot liquid glass on its end. The glass was then carefully shaped with special tools and cooled until it was hard. Today, glassblowing survives mostly as an art form.

Spreading the Word

Thomas Edison knew that in order to sell his light bulbs he had to let people everywhere know about his invention. When J. P. Morgan and the Vanderbilts first invested in this invention, they expected Edison to develop a product that would make money.

Most people of the time were not familiar with electric lighting, except for arc lamps. The dangers of electricity and wires, moreover, were a little frightening to the public. Still, Edison hoped to make his newly improved light bulb something that people would want to use in their homes and businesses. On December 21, 1879, he ran the first public notice about the incandescent light bulb in the *New York Herald*.

Edison also wanted people to see firsthand what his light bulb could do. On New Year's Eve in 1879, more than 3,000 people came to Menlo Park to see the laboratory illuminated with twenty-five warmly glowing incandescent light bulbs. This event was the first of many to present electric lighting to the public.

Edison was very famous and was frequently featured in the press.

Before electric lights, every evening at dusk, street lighters had to light the gas lamps that lined city streets.

The SS *Columbia* was the first commercial user of Edison's light bulb. At night it was brightly illuminated by 150 lights.

In 1880, Edison had another opportunity to advertise the light bulb. One of his financial supporters, Henry Villard, asked him to furnish the new steamship SS *Columbia* with electric lighting. As the ship sailed around South America, people at each port came to see the magically lit boat.

However, Edison faced a setback that same year when Joseph Swan sued him for using his light bulb design, which was patented. The British courts ruled in Swan's favor. They believed that Swan should receive money and recognition for his design from Edison. Edison was required to make Swan a partner in his British electric works. The company was renamed the Edison and Swan United Electric Company.

Although Swan was the one to receive the patent for the light bulb, Edison improved it dramatically. He created a light bulb that was easy to use and affordable for the average person. His achievement changed the world.

This sketch was prepared for a sign showing Edison's name in lights. The inventor produced the sign and displayed it at the Crystal Palace in London.

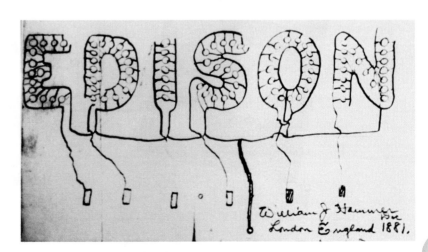

Powering the Light Bulb

The dramatic lighting of the SS *Columbia* was a huge success. It helped to spark the public's interest in incandescent lighting.

It also allowed Edison to turn his attention to designing electric power sources and ways to deliver power to customers. The electricity for the SS *Columbia* was generated by a single plant on the bottom floor of the ship. Edison's main interest, however, was to develop central plants, which could deliver electricity to widely scattered areas.

early electric meter

The inventor began to map out a plan for delivering electricity to the general population. First, Edison created a meter, based on the design of existing gas meters, to measure electricity usage. People could then be billed for the exact amount of power they used. Second, Edison's team used a network of wires to carry the electricity from a central plant to its customers.

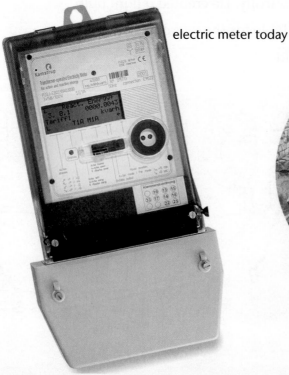

electric meter today

laying electrical tubes in the 1880s

The Edison team worked around the clock, often sleeping only three or four hours each night. They had to create powerful generators to make the electricity. Lighting fixtures, safety switches, and fuse boxes were invented along with other items. Edison also continued to improve the light bulb itself, looking for longer-lasting and cheaper materials.

As the initial planning drew to a close, Edison decided that a section of Lower Manhattan in New York City called the First District would be a good place to install his first large electric plant. Edison chose New York City because many of his investors were there, and he thought the city would be a good location to show how a delivery system connected to a central plant worked.

the generator for Edison's first electric plant

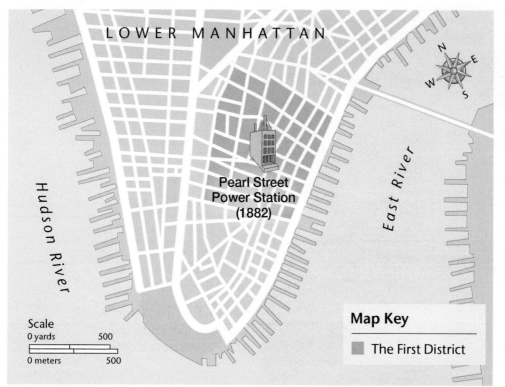

LOWER MANHATTAN

Hudson River

East River

Pearl Street Power Station (1882)

Scale
0 yards   500
0 meters   500

Map Key

The First District

Pearl Street Station began with one generator, which produced power for 800 electric light bulbs. Within 14 months, over 12,000 bulbs were aglow. However, with Edison's direct current system, the voltage dropped as distance from the generator increased. Plants had to be built close to users. This was costly and soon led to the development of better systems by rival companies.

137

The Pearl Street Power Station

The power station was a huge undertaking. First, a location was chosen for the huge steam generators that would make the electricity. The team decided on Pearl Street in Lower Manhattan. Then wires were laced along telegraph poles, and holes were dug in the city streets for underground cables to deliver the electricity. Finally, the First District's buildings themselves were wired.

On September 4, 1882, Edison flipped a switch in J. P. Morgan's office. For the first time, electric power flowed to the homes and businesses of the First District, setting the neighborhood aglow with incandescent light.

By the end of the 1880s, electric lights were being used 24 hours a day, particularly for transportation and business needs. Edison had proved that his power and electric lighting system could work on a large scale. The inventor told a newspaper reporter, "I have accomplished all I promised." In the United States, the name Edison Electric Light Company would later be changed to General Electric.

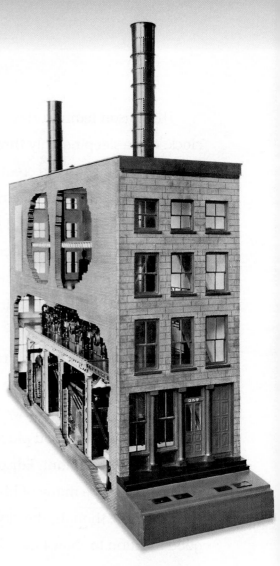

model of the Pearl Street Power Station in New York City

Roads in the First District were dug up so that underground cables could be laid down.

Generating Power

A generator converts the energy of motion into electricity through a process called electromagnetic induction. The process involves the following steps.

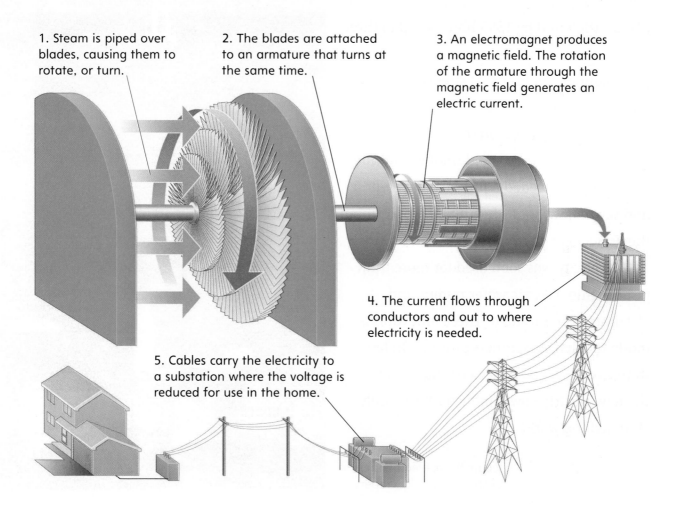

1. Steam is piped over blades, causing them to rotate, or turn.

2. The blades are attached to an armature that turns at the same time.

3. An electromagnet produces a magnetic field. The rotation of the armature through the magnetic field generates an electric current.

4. The current flows through conductors and out to where electricity is needed.

5. Cables carry the electricity to a substation where the voltage is reduced for use in the home.

Portable Generators

Some early generators were small enough to be pulled by horses to the location where a power source was needed. This generator, made by Charles Parsons, was used in England to light up a pond for night skating.

Electricity Changes the World

From 1879 to 1882, the number of customers that used Thomas Edison's light bulbs totaled 203. That number increased to 710 by 1889 and by 1899 had soared to three million customers.

Incandescent lights set streets, hospitals, schools, and offices aglow. People began to make huge changes in the way they lived. After dark they could finally continue activities that needed light, such as reading and sewing, without eyestrain or worry about the dangers of gas explosions.

Electricity was soon used for more than just lighting. Electric water pumps and elevators were invented. These innovations made the first skyscrapers possible. In less than twenty years, the electric light and the new electric power industry had totally changed the world.

Electricity enabled builders to construct huge skyscrapers.

Edison's Death

Thomas Edison died on October 18, 1931, at the age of eighty-four. President Herbert Hoover asked U.S. citizens to dim their lights at ten o'clock that evening in honor of the great inventor.

THE DAILY MIRROR   Monday, October 19, 1931

EDISON, THE WORLD'S GREATEST INVENTOR, DEAD

GENIUS WHOSE DISCOVERIES
TRANSFORMED OUR LIVES

Made Electricity, Moving Pictures and Telephones Realities to All

Thomas Alva Edison, the greatest inventor the world has ever known, died early yesterday at his home in West Orange, New Jersey, U.S.A., aged eighty-four.

Electricity in the Home

One major factor slowed the placing of electric lights in homes: the cost of installing wiring. However, people became more willing to invest in wiring when they realized it would allow for many conveniences in addition to lighting. At the end of the nineteenth and beginning of the twentieth centuries, all kinds of electric appliances were being invented.

Many electric inventions made housework easier and life more pleasant. Personal grooming appliances started to appear. Electric heaters and fans were introduced to control temperature. Today, new or improved electric appliances for the home are invented every year.

Electric Invention	Year Invented
Iron	1882
Fan	1886
Hairdryer	1890
Stove	1891
Toaster	1893
Washing machine	1908
Electric heating	1916

tea maker

In the early twentieth century, many different kinds of electric gadgets, such as those shown here, were invented.

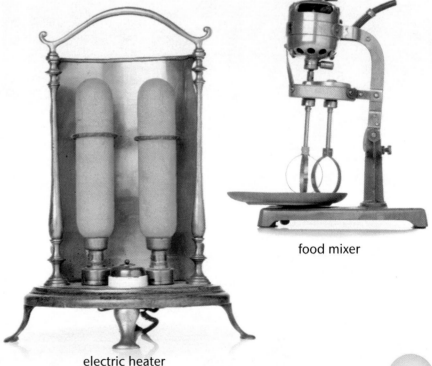

electric heater

food mixer

Lighting Today

Since the days of Edison, light fixtures and bulbs have continued to evolve. In 1910, the American inventor William Coolidge improved on the General Electric Company's method of making tungsten light bulb filaments. Because of its high melting point, tungsten has turned out to be the best filament material yet discovered. With Coolidge's improvements, tungsten became more affordable. Today, most light bulbs have tungsten filaments.

Fluorescent and neon light bulbs are also available. Instead of using a filament within a vacuum, an electric current is passed through a low-pressure gas. The energy of the current is converted to light by gas atoms. Fluorescent and neon bulbs provide as much light as incandescent bulbs, yet they use less electricity. French scientist Alexandre Edmond Becquerel first created fluorescent bulbs in 1867. They were not introduced to the public, however, until the New York World's Fair of 1938–1939.

Halogen lamps are incandescent lights that have a tungsten filament. The presence of halogen in the bulb allows the filament to run at a higher temperature than in a conventional bulb, so the light is brighter.

Neon lights are used mostly for advertisements. The color of the light depends on the type of gas inside the bulb.

143

Energy and the Environment

Today, lighting and appliances create huge demands for electric power. Think about how many inventions, including cars, refrigerators, and ovens, use light bulbs.

As a result, great amounts of fossil fuels are burned to generate electricity. Fossil fuels are nonrenewable energy sources because once they are burned, they are hard to replace. Moreover, carbon dioxide gas is released into the air, which contributes to global warming.

Wind, water, and solar power are renewable energy sources because they do not get used up in the same way as fossil fuels, such as oil and coal, do. All over the world, people are trying to develop ways to use these power sources instead of fossil fuels. Hydroelectric dams, for example, use moving water to generate power.

Solar panels are used to gather sunlight and turn the radiant energy into heat or electric energy. Solar power is a clean and practically limitless energy source. However, it is still costly to use in comparison to coal and oil.

Wind farms generate electricity without damaging the environment.

Hydroelectric dams use water
to generate electricity.

The electricity that hydroelectric dams generate is no different than electricity made from fossil fuels. Yet these dams do not produce the emissions that come from burning fossil fuels. However, hydroelectric dams can present their own threats to the environment by affecting water flow rates and water temperatures.

Careful planning must be used no matter what kind of power source is developed. When the world finds more ways to use renewable energy sources, Earth will become a much cleaner and healthier planet.

No one knows exactly what light sources will be used in the future. One thing, however, is certain: People will always want more light in their lives, especially once the Sun has set.

From Fire to the Light Bulb: A Timeline

3000 B.C. and earlier

The Sun, Moon, and fire are the main light sources until torches and stone lamps appear.

3000 B.C.–2000 B.C.

Wicks and candles are invented.

about 600 B.C.

The Greek mathematician Thales experiments with static electricity.

1800

Alessandro Volta of Italy creates the first battery, called the Voltaic Pile.

1809

Humphry Davy pioneers arc lighting in London, England.

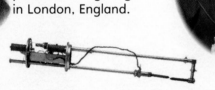

1820

Warren de la Rue makes the first light bulb in London, England.

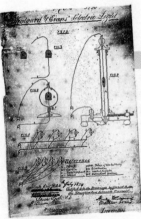

1874

Henry Woodward and Matthew Evans patent their light bulb in Canada.

1878

- Joseph Swan patents his incandescent light bulb.
- Edison Electric Light Company is founded in the United States.

1879

Thomas Edison introduces his incandescent light bulb.

1600s

Improvements are made in oil lamps and candles.

1700s

- William Murdock of Scotland uses coal gas to light his home and his company's factory.
- The Leyden jar is developed in the Netherlands.
- Benjamin Franklin experiments with electricity and invents the lightning rod in the United States.

1823

London streets are illuminated with gas lamps.

1841

Frederick de Moleyns of England receives the first light bulb patent.

1867

Alexandre Edmond Becquerel of France invents the fluorescent light bulb.

1880

Thomas Edison supplies an electric light system for the American ship SS *Columbia*.

1882

Thomas Edison opens the first electric power station in New York City.

1910

William Coolidge improves the tungsten filament, making its production more affordable.

What Is Coding, Anyway?

By James Floyd Kelly

We live in a digital world surrounded by technology. It's not just the advanced phones and tablets that provide us with a constant connection to others or the modern toys, games, and gadgets that we use. It's also the alarm clocks and toasters that help us begin our day. It's even the traffic lights that control our trips to school or work. Electronic devices are an integral part of our lives, even if most of us don't completely understand how they work.

Hardware

If you take apart just about any electronic device, you'll find a number of components that might make you scratch your head. These components include resistors, capacitors, microchips (also known as integrated circuits), LEDs (light-emitting diodes), speakers, and motors. When put together, these physical parts make up the hardware. Hardware is the phone you hold in your hand, the television you watch, or the speakers that play your music. Hardware is what you can touch and see and hear.

This disassembled phone shows all the components that make up the hardware.

Software

Inside almost every electronic device is an invisible component. Without it, the device would never function in the first place. Software, sometimes referred to as a device's program, goes hand in hand with hardware to make each gadget work. When you press the home button on a tablet, the screen turns on. The tablet's software makes that happen.

Just as certain skills are needed to assemble the hardware to make a working electronic device, special skills are required to create its software. People who create software are called programmers. Programming skills are in high demand as our world's reliance on technology continues to increase. The exciting part is that anyone can learn these skills.

Without software, a gaming console is pretty useless!

A program is a set of instructions that guide an electronic device to function properly and perform tasks correctly.

When a programmer finishes writing software, the program can be run (or executed) and tested for errors (or debugged). Any errors or mistakes in the instructions are corrected. Then the program is tested again for bugs. When the program is determined to be complete and free of errors, it can then be uploaded to a device or sold as an application for a smartphone, tablet, or computer.

Software can be as simple as the temperature conversion program on this page. Or it can be as complex as the programs that manage incoming and outgoing flights at a busy airport or keep the International Space Station in orbit around Earth.

```cpp
int main()
{
    float c_temp, f_temp;

    cout << "Enter Celsius temperature";
    cin >> c_temp; // input from the user

    f_temp = (c_temp * 1.8) + 32; // convert to Fahrenheit

    cout << "Fahrenheit temperature: " << f_temp << endl;

    return 0;
}
```

This simple computer program is a set of instructions for converting temperatures from Celsius to Fahrenheit. First, the user inputs a temperature measured in degrees Celsius. Then, computer solves a mathematical equation. Finally, it provides the equivalent temperature in degrees Fahrenheit.

Algorithms and Code

Programs and software are examples of algorithms. In simple terms, an algorithm is a step-by-step procedure. A cake recipe, for example, is an algorithm for baking a cake. If you carefully follow the algorithm, then you should end up with a delicious cake. The same thing goes for an electronic device, such as a smartphone. When the phone's hardware follows the instructions in the software, the phone will ring or vibrate when a call or text is received.

Ant Algorithms?

Most people think of computers when they think of algorithms. But algorithms are also found throughout nature. Researchers have recently discovered that some kinds of ants that forage for food use algorithms. These instructions are used to control the flow of ants leaving the colony in search of food, based on the number of ants with food coming into the colony. One of the researchers even found that the ant algorithm is similar to one used in some Internet technologies to control the flow of data!

If an algorithm is a procedure or set of instructions, then code is the language used to write the instructions. Code is a symbolic language, or a language made up of symbols. Have you ever created a language using symbols to write secret messages to friends, such as the one here? Then you've used code.

Code Key

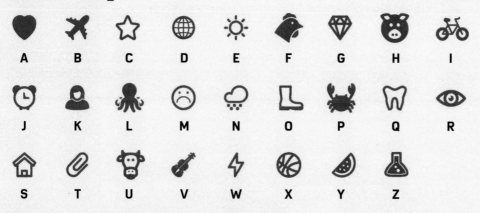

Secret Message

In this code, each letter of the alphabet is represented by a different symbol. If you know the code, then you can write and read secret messages. Can you figure out what the secret message says?

Coding is the term given to creating a program. Most often it involves typing commands, in a specific order, into special software that allows programmers to save, edit, and test their programs.

Just as there are many spoken languages throughout the world, there are thousands of coding languages that programmers use to create instructions. The languages may look and behave differently. However, they all share a common goal—to allow a programmer to create software, such as applications (or apps), that provides special functionality to a digital device.

Coding or Programming?

Today, the terms *coding* and *programming* are often used interchangeably. However, *coding* is sometimes used to describe a task performed by novice programmers who might be modifying an existing program or just tinkering with a program to learn how it works. Most professionals use the term *programming* to describe the creation of a complete application, from start to finish. The difference between *coding* and *programming*, however, is becoming blurred as more and more people learn to program—or code.

DNA: The Code of Life

Every organism—plant or animal—contains DNA. This genetic information allows an organism to function and live. DNA, which is located within every cell in an organism, is shaped like a twisted ladder. The information in it is coded using four different chemical bases that pair up to make the rungs of the ladder. All the instructions our cells need to perform their functions are coded with just these four bases.

How Has Coding Evolved?

Early coding languages consisted of simple command words such as GOTO, STOP, and INPUT. One programming language called BASIC (Beginner's All-Purpose Symbolic Instruction Code) even required that commands be performed in a particular order by adding numbered lines for each command.

As technology has expanded, so has the number of coding and programming languages. There is probably no accurate count of the number of programming languages that exist today. Simple coding languages are taught to young children. Complex languages are taught in many colleges and universities. Many special languages are developed by companies for their own private use too.

This simple BASIC program instructs the computer to print onscreen the three lines of text over and over. The result of the program is shown immediately below it.

```
10 PRINT "Hello, Programmer!"
20 PRINT "This is an example of a program loop."
30 PRINT "This text will repeat over and over..."
40 GOTO 10
RUN

Hello, Programmer!
This is an example of a program loop.
This text will repeat over and over...
Hello, Programmer!
This is an example of a program loop.
This text will repeat over and over...
Hello, Programmer!
This is an example of a program loop.
This text will repeat over and over...
```

You wouldn't try giving instructions in English to someone who only speaks Japanese, would you? Coding languages are the same. Different languages are used for different purposes and systems. For example, an older programming language called COBOL (Common Business-Oriented Language) was developed in 1959. It was used by businesses to develop applications that assist with complex financial tasks. FORTRAN 77 (Formula Translating System) is another older language that was used by researchers, engineers, and mathematicians. This language was good at handling complex equations.

This code written in Python calculates the cost of buying oranges and peaches at the supermarket and then displays the total.

prices of fruit

calculation of purchase

```
prices = {'orange': 0.40, 'peach': 0.60}

my_purchase = {
                'orange': 1,
                'peach': 6}
market_bill = sum(prices[fruit] * my_purchase[fruit]
            for fruit in my_purchase)

print 'I owe $%.2f' % market_bill
```

display of total cost

Specialty languages continue to be developed today. Scratch (developed at MIT in 2003) is a visual programming language created to appeal to young students who can create programs by "snapping together" color-coded elements.

Some companies have developed special tools just for designing games. Users can create simple or complex games by dragging characters, obstacles, enemies, and other elements onto the screen with a mouse. As with Scratch, the coding portion is graphical and can be learned quickly using built-in tutorials and onscreen help features.

Complex programming languages that require more training include Python, Ruby, and C++. Python is typical of most programming languages in many ways. It is text-based, and many of the command words may be recognizable (such as WHILE or PRINT). But other portions can look like a cryptic mix of special symbols such as * ! = %.

Scratch programming language, developed by the Lifelong Kindergarten Group at the MIT Media Lab, allows users to create animations, games, and interactive stories using simple pieces of code that snap together. In this workspace, for example, you can write code to make the cat sprite, or character, move around on the screen.

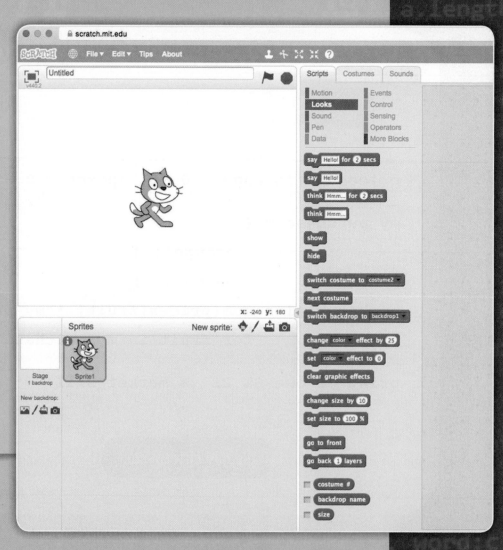

In Scratch, the user drags "blocks" of instructions to the right.

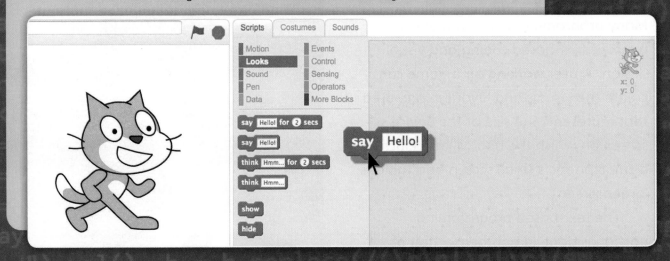

As the user adds more instructions, they "snap" together to combine scripts.

When the user has assembled the code sequence, the results play out in the Stage area to the left.

Learning to Code

Many programming environments are a mix of text-based coding and visual design. A user working on a game can create the visuals and layout in one area that represents the size of the device's screen on which the app will run (such as a smartphone's small screen or a tablet's larger screen).

The text-based programming portion is done in another section of the environment. The programmer selects single elements on the screen (for example, the game's scoreboard) and writes small snippets of text-based code that are specific to the selected element. All of the game's various elements (for example, scoreboard, characters, and timer) and their behind-the-scenes code work together to present a complete game to the player.

As with many new skills, coding can be learned using a variety of methods. Colleges and universities typically offer advanced programming classes. Many middle schools and high schools provide students with their first exposure to programming. And while books have often been a favored method for learning a new programming tool, another approach for novices wishing to learn to code are free online courses. More recently, a new concept for teaching programming has appeared. In so-called coding boot camps, people enroll in a class and receive training in a programming language for anywhere from one to three months.

Microcontrollers are found in many everyday products, including games and toys. They allow the user to program the gadget to perform almost any function they can think of!

Kids and Coding

Today's young students have access to a wide range of tools when it comes to learning how to code. With some programming skills under their belts, students may find an amazing array of projects and opportunities available to them.

Some online sites offer students the chance to learn to program games that they can then modify and make available for their friends to play. Students can continue their training by creating apps to remotely control toys and robots.

For young people interested in both hardware and software, there's no better tool than a microcontroller.

Designed for novices, these mini-computers can be used to control motors, LEDs, and other components that connect to an electronic device. A simple coding language is also available to write programs that can be uploaded to the device to control the connected hardware. Students all over the world have created robots, special sensors to monitor air quality, and other amazing tools and gadgets.

In recent years, some creative students have become successful entrepreneurs by developing programs and apps. A computer doesn't care about your age or education level, so anyone can learn how to code and create the next major app. Maybe even you!

a microcontroller

You Don't Need a Computer to Code!

How can you use code to create an algorithm without a computer? With a small group, try the following activity in which you will instruct a robot to complete a simple task.

Robot Program

Materials: five wooden blocks per team, index cards, pen or pencil

1. Assign roles to team members:
   - Two or more students are the software developers. They will write a set of instructions to build a figure using five wooden blocks.
   - Another team member is the coder. That student will translate the software developers' instructions using only the four symbols shown below.
   - Another student is the robot arm, whose job is to carry out the actions that the code describes.

2. The coders and robots from all the teams should study the symbols while the developers write their instructions.

Pick up block **Put down and release block** **Move right one step (half block width to the right)**   **Move left one step (half block width to the left)**

3. The developers should decide on a figure to build with the blocks without the robot seeing what it is. The developers should then write a simple set of instructions that explains how to build the figure. For example: "Pick up block. Move right one step. Move right one step. Put down and release block." And so on.

4. Each coder should take the instructions written by his or her team's developers and translate them using the four symbols only. The coder writes the symbols on an index card with the code for moving each block, using a separate row for each block.

5. When the coders in each team have finished their programs, they should stack the blocks on the table for their team robots.

6. Each robot should return to its team and "run," or act out, the program by following the symbols on the index card. (When the robot arm picks up a block from the stack, the block will always be raised higher than the highest block in the figure, so there's no need for a simple "up" code.)

7. The coder and developers should observe the robot's actions, making sure the instructions are followed correctly. If team members notice a mistake, then the team should debug the program. Teams should identify and correct any errors in the code. Have the robot run the program again.

8. Once the robot has successfully run the program, each team can create more figures using the blocks and challenge other teams to code the program for building their figures.

Before doing the activity with your own five-block figure, look at the example on the next page.

Now you're coding without a computer!

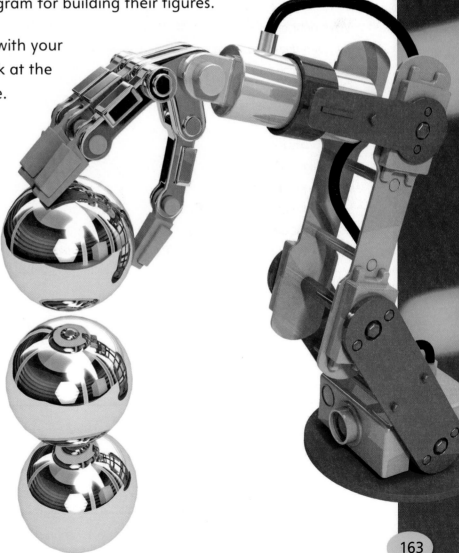

Robotic arms, like the one simulated in this activity, are used to manufacture everything from automobiles to microprocessors.

Example

Suppose the robot arm is building this figure using only three wooden blocks.

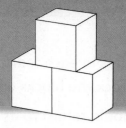

This diagram shows how many steps are needed to move each block from the stack to build the figure. Remember that each step right or left moves the block a distance of ½ the width of a block.

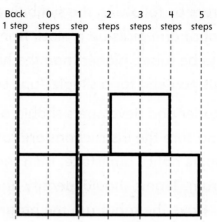

The instructions and code for the robot to build the figure are:

Pick up *block.*
Move right one *step.*
Move right one *step.*
Put down and release *block.*
Move left one *step.*
Move left one *step.*

Pick up *block.*
Move right one *step.*
Move right one *step.*
Move right one *step.*
Move right one *step.*
Put down and release *block.*
Move left one *step.*
Move left one *step.*
Move left one *step.*
Move left one *step.*

Pick up *block.*
Move right one *step.*
Move right one *step.*
Move right one *step.*
Put down and release *block.*
Move left one *step.*
Move left one *step.*
Move left one *step.*

algorithm a step-by-step procedure to complete a task

bug an error or mistake in the coding of a program or software

code a language of symbols used to write a program

debug to test a program for errors in the code

execute to run a program

hardware the physical components that make up an electronic device

program a set of instructions written in code that guide an electronic device to function properly and perform tasks correctly; software

software a set of instructions written in code that guide an electronic device to function properly and perform tasks correctly; program

sprite a computer graphic that can be moved around onscreen

symbolic language a language made up of symbols

COMING SOON

TO A HOSPITAL NEAR YOU!

3D Printing Lands a Leading Role in Medicine

by Kristina Lyn Heitkamp

Medical three-dimensional printing is about to blow your mind! But don't worry. In the future you might be able to print a replacement.

Medical 3D printing is similar to regular 2D printing. But instead of using ink on a piece of paper, 3D printing uses plastic, metals, and even human cells as ink. Layer by layer, the three-dimensional object is created, whether it's a replica of a dog's skull or a human ear.

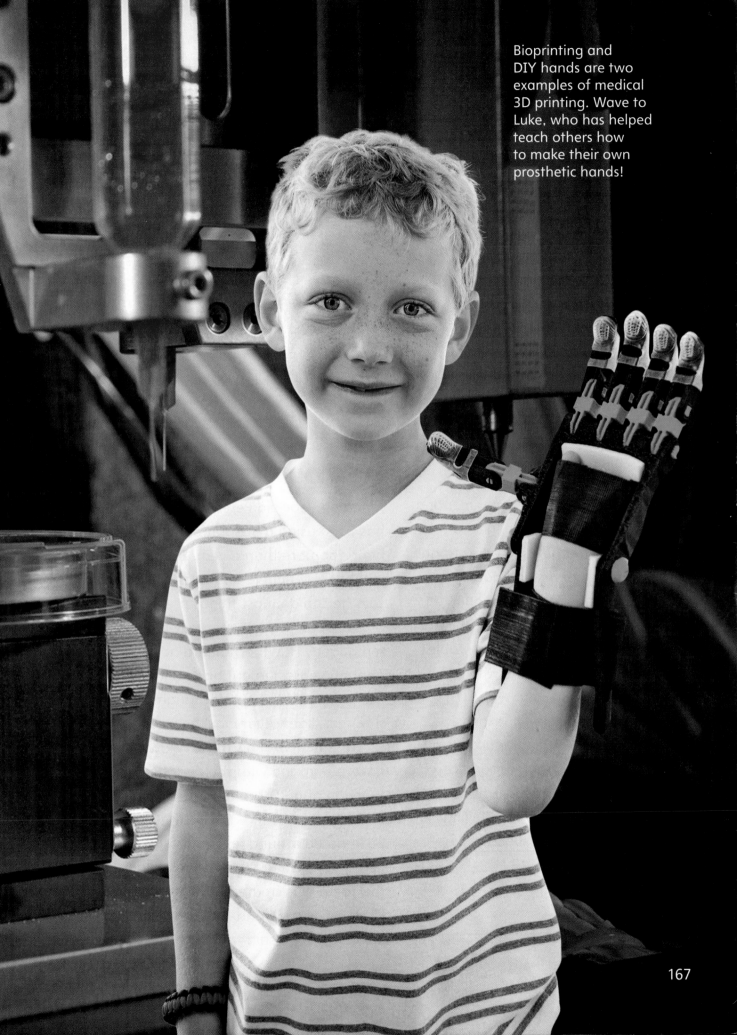

Bioprinting and DIY hands are two examples of medical 3D printing. Wave to Luke, who has helped teach others how to make their own prosthetic hands!

167

Scientists, engineers, and enthusiasts have been experimenting with medical 3D printing in a variety of ways, from producing educational models for students and doctors to practice on and study to printing parts of a prosthetic hand that can be assembled on your kitchen table.

Prosthetics can come with a hefty ticket price, but with 3D printing, materials are inexpensive and the prosthetic easily customized. With the low cost, a new hand can be made when needed—say, if a finger gets busted from playing basketball or after a sudden growth spurt.

Introducing Talon

Nineteen-year-old Peregrine Hawthorn has been using a 3D-printed prosthetic hand for more than a year. Born without any fingers on his left hand, he says he can do most things pretty well— but for some things you really need all ten fingers. Hawthorn heard about 3D printing years ago but had no idea how useful it could be. "I just thought it was this neat, sciencey thing," he said.

Together with his father, Hawthorn tinkered around with the design and function of a 3D-printed prosthetic. He knew he wanted a hand that could be knocked around, especially during heavy yard work. $50 in supplies later, the Talon was created. "Plus the Talon looks really cool, and that's always important," he said.

There are still some things Hawthorn can't do with the Talon, like lift more than ten pounds. Plus wearing the hand can be tiring and strain his arm. But there is always room for improvement. Hawthorn is part of the group e-NABLE: a global network of engineers, medical professionals, students, and parents who collaborate and volunteer to design and make 3D-printed prosthetics.

Blockbuster Technology

Slipping on a prosthetic hand or studying a printed human jawbone is just scratching the surface of possibilities with medical 3D printing. Wake Forest Institute for Regenerative Medicine located in Winston-Salem, North Carolina, began experimenting with the technology. They have bioprinted a three-dimensional model of a kidney.

Bioprinting is similar to regular 3D printing, but instead of plastic it uses live human cells to build a functional living organ. The patient's own cells are used, so the printed organ is compatible and chance of rejection is slim to none. Then the cells are bioprinted in a very specific order, built from the ground up or with the assistance of a 3D-printed scaffold or mold in the shape of the organ.

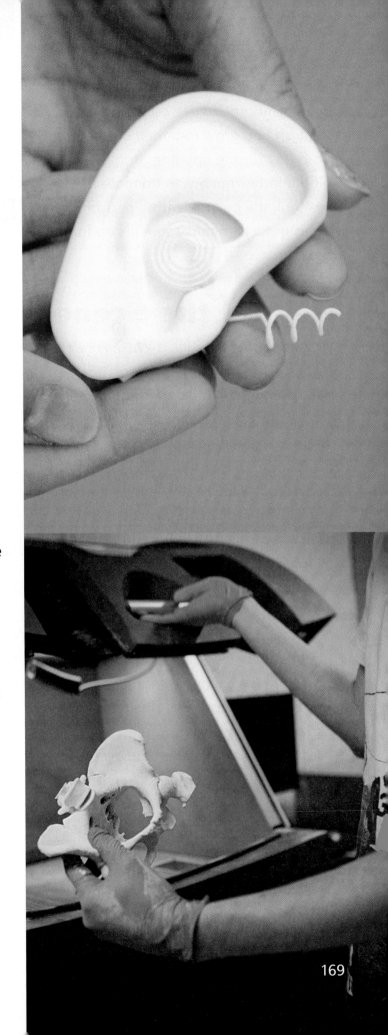

After printing, the organ is placed in an incubator, where cells have time to mesh and grow together. But before it's ready for the operating table, the bioprinted organ has to do more than just look the part. Scientists perform a series of tests to make sure it's up for the job.

Dr. Aleksander Skardal

Behind the Scenes

Dr. Aleksander Skardal, a Wake Forest Institute scientist and professor, has been working with bioprinting for more than eight years. He says it's been wildly interesting building organs from scratch. His favorite bioprinting project is the Body-on-a-Chip. "We are bioprinting small, even microscopic, versions of different organs. Then we connect them all together on a microchip, which lets us model the human body on a tiny microchip," he said. They use the Body-on-a-Chip to test the effectiveness and safety of new medicines.

Another exciting development is the Skin Bioprinting project. "We're printing skin cells onto wounds. Researchers on our team have developed a machine that can bioprint new cells directly onto a person's hurt part of the body. These cells then turn into new skin over time," Skardal said. He hopes this technology will eventually be used in hospitals.

Stay Tuned . . .

Libraries across the United States are beginning to offer 3D printing. You can even buy a small 3D printer at the local hardware store. With easier access, the question of what's next tickles the minds of many. The opportunity to print workable parts, whether plastic or living, could produce a future of robohands and lab-grown ears. It could mean no more organ donor waiting lists. But if you could bioprint a human heart, what's next? A brain? Think about it.

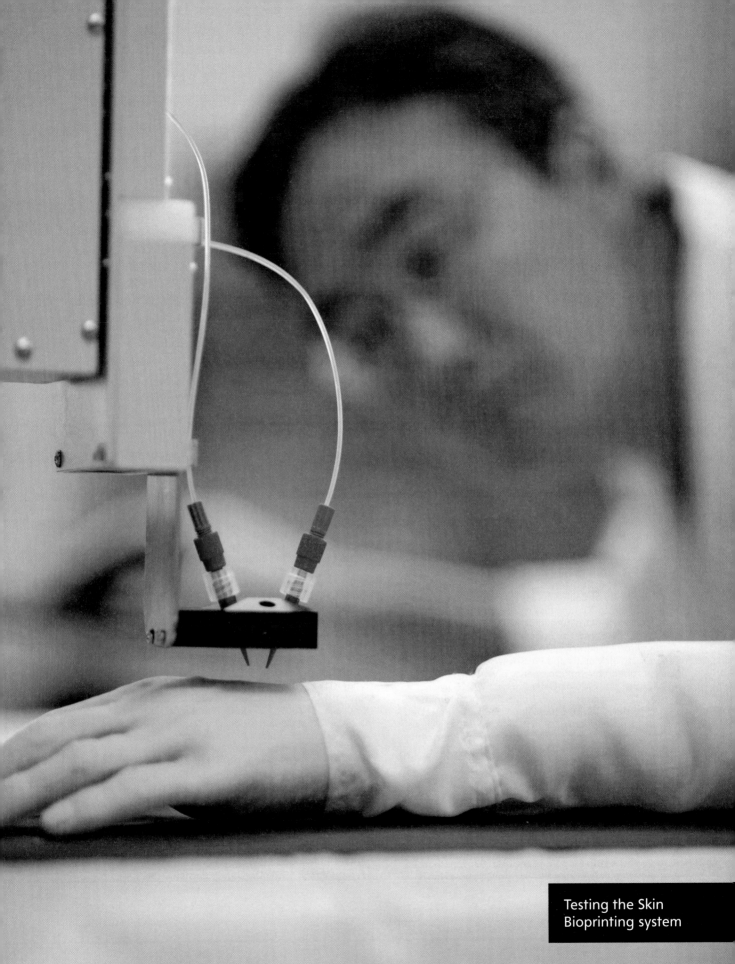

Testing the Skin
Bioprinting system

Text

Reprinted with permission of Simon & Schuster Books for Young Readers, an imprint of Simon & Schuster Children's Publishing Division from THE INVISIBLE THREAD by Yoshiko Uchida. Copyright © Yoshiko Uchida.

No Vacany by Katherine Carlman is reprinted with the permission of publisher *Plays, The Drama Magazine for Young People*/Sterling Partners Inc.

Excerpted from the work entitled *Gadgets and Games* by Chris Oxlade. Copyright © 2013 Capstone Press. Used by permission of Capstone Press. All rights reserved.

"Screen Time Can Mess With the Body's 'Clock'," by Andrew Bridges. Reprinted with permission of Science News for Students.

"Coming Soon to a Hospital Near You" by Kristina Lyn Heitkamp. © by Carus Publishing Company. Reproduced with permission. All Cricket Media material is copyrighted by Carus Publishing Company, d/b/a Cricket Media, and/or various authors and illustrators. Any commercial use or distribution of material without permission is strictly prohibited. Please visit cricketmedia.com for licensing and subscriptions.

Images

Photo locators denoted as follows: Top (T), Center (C), Bottom (B), Left (L), Right (R), Background (Bkgd)

4Bkgd: Franzi/Shutterstock; **5:** Courtesy of The Bancroft Library University of California, Berkeley; **6:** Courtesy of The Bancroft Library University of California, Berkeley; **18:** Mapping Specialists; **24:** Courtesy of The Bancroft Library University of California, Berkeley; **26TL:** George Fry/Courtesy of The Bancroft Library University of California, Berkeley; **26TR:** Patrick McMullan Co./Crotty/McMullan/Sipa Press/Newscom; **26BL:** Epa european pressphoto agency b.v./Alamy; **26BR:** Mark Mainz/Getty Images; **27:** Courtesy of The Bancroft Library University of California, Berkeley; **28L:** DJ Dates/Alamy; **28R:** The Protected Art Archive/Alamy; **29:** Nsf/Alamy; **30–31:** Nsf/Alamy; **31:** George Fry/Courtesy of The Bancroft Library University of California, Berkeley; **32:** Patrick McMullan Co./Crotty/McMullan/Sipa Press/Newscom; **33:** ZUMA Press/Alamy; **35:** Agencia el Universal GDA Photo Service/Newscom; **36:** Epa european pressphoto agency b.v./Alamy; **37:** University Hospitals Birmingham/AP Images; **38:** Epa european pressphoto agency b.v./Alamy; **39:** Epa european pressphoto agency b.v./Alamy; **40:** Mark Mainz/Getty Images; **41:** Wendy Stone/Corbis; **41BR:** Mapping Specialist; **43:** Jonathan Ernst/Reuters/Corbis; **44–45:** Amy Nichole Harris/Shutterstock; **46–53:** Susan Keeter; **54:** Alexander Caminada/Alamy; **55:** Jurgen Schadeberg/Getty Images; **57:** Anesh Debiky/AFP/Getty Images; **58:** Christie's Images/Fine Art Premium/Corbis; **60:** Christin Gilbert/Age Fotostock/SuperStock; **63(Arrow):** Elina Li/Shutterstock; **63L:** Andrew Buckin/Shutterstock; **63TR:** Interfoto/Alamy; **63BR:** Scyther5/Shutterstock; **66T:** Phant/Shutterstock; **66BL:** Cobalt88/Shutterstock; **66BR:** Oleksandr Kazmirchuk/123RF; **67T:** Tele52/Shutterstock; **67BL:** Tele52/Shutterstock; **67BR:** Tele52/Shutterstock; **69T:** Cobalt/123RF; **69B:** Jay P. Morgan/Stockbyte/Getty Images; **70:** Look Die Bildagentur der Fotografen GmbH/Alamy; **72:** SPi Global; **73:** Hugh Threlfall/Alamy; **75:** Ingo Bartussek/Fotolia; **76:** SPi Global; **77:** Courtesy of iFixit; **78:** OJO Images Ltd/Alamy; **80:** Ton Koene/Age Fotostock/SuperStock; **81:** Alex Mit/Shutterstock; **82:** David Stock/Alamy; **83T:** Leenvdb/Shutterstock; **83B:** Nnv/Fotolia; **84:** Oliver Berg/Dpa/Corbis; **86:** SPi Global; **87:** Studiomode/Alamy; **88:** Dmitry Vereshchagin/Fotolia; **89:** Ryan McGinnis/Alamy; **90:** Qilai Shen/In Pictures/Corbis; **91–92:** SPi Global; **93:** Leo Ramirez/AFP/Getty Images; **94:** Daniel Boschung/Media Bakery; **95:** James Blinn/Alamy; **96:** Park Ji-Hwan/AFP/Getty Images; **97:** Rangizzz/Shutterstock; **98:** Oli Scarff/Getty Images; **100:** Blazej Lyjak/Shutterstock; **101:** Sean Yong/Reuters/Corbis; **103T:** Olga Drabovich/Shutterstock; **103B:** Makhnach_S/Shutterstock; **104:** Issouf Sanogo/AFP/Getty Images; **105:** Cobalt/123RF; **106:** Jerry Mason/Science Source; **107:** Nelsonart/Deposit Photos; **108–111Bkgd:** Optimarc/Shutterstock; **112–113:** Adam121/Fotolia; **114–115:** Jasmin Merdan/Fotolia; **116Bkgd:** Nigel Hicks/Dorling Kindersley Ltd.; **116:** Dorling Kindersley © 2005; **117:** Jörg Hackemann/Fotolia; **118–119:** Dorling Kindersley © 2005; **120T:** Dorling Kindersley © 2005; **120C:** Dorling Kindersley © 2005; **120BL:** Dorling Kindersley © 2005; **120BR:** Logan Carter/Shutterstock; **121:** Dorling Kindersley © 2005; **122T:** Ristoviitanen/Fotolia; **122B:** Library of Congress; **123T:** Dorling Kindersley © 2005; **123B:** Dorling Kindersley © 2005; **124L:** Dorling Kindersley © 2005; **124R:** Zadiraka Vladislav/Fotolia; **125T:** Nickolae/Fotolia; **125BL:** Dorling Kindersley © 2005; **125BR:** Dorling Kindersley © 2005; **126L:** Dorling Kindersley © 2005; **126R:** Cherkas/Fotolia; **127T:** V&A Images/Alamy; **127B:** Dorling Kindersley © 2005; **128T:** Dorling Kindersley © 2005; **128B:** Library of Congress; **129T:** Pictorial Press Ltd./Alamy; **129BL:** Dave King/Dorling Kindersley Ltd.; **129BR:** Dorling Kindersley © 2005; **130T:** Library of Congress; **130B:** Library of Congress; **131:** Dorling Kindersley Ltd.; **132L:** Dorling Kindersley © 2005; **132R:** Dorling Kindersley © 2005; **133T:** Dorling Kindersley © 2005; **133B:** Johnny Franzen/Getty Images; **134T:** Dorling Kindersley © 2005; **134B:** Interfoto/History/Alamy; **135T:** Dorling Kindersley © 2005;

135B: Dorling Kindersley © 2005; **136T:** Dorling Kindersley © 2005; **136BL:** Dorling Kindersley © 2005; **136BR:** W.P. Snyder. /Library of Congress; **137:** Library of Congress; **138T:** Dorling Kindersley © 2005; **138B:** Dorling Kindersley © 2005; **139:** Science and Society/SuperStock; **140T:** Rabbit75_fot/Fotolia; **140B:** Dorling Kindersley © 2005; **141L:** Dave King/Dorling Kindersley Ltd.; **141C:** Dave King/Dorling Kindersley Ltd.; **141R:** Dave King/Dorling Kindersley Ltd.; **142–143:** Nigel Hicks/Dorling Kindersley Ltd.; **144:** Pedrosala/Fotolia; **145:** BirgitMundtOsterwiec/Fotolia; **146:** Andy/Fotolia; **147:** F9photos/Fotolia; **148TL:** Dorling Kindersley © 2005; **148TR:** Dorling Kindersley © 2005; **148CL:** Nickolae/Fotolia; **148C:** Dorling Kindersley © 2005; **148CR:** V&A Images/Alamy; **148BL:** Dorling Kindersley © 2005; **148BC:** Dave King/Dorling Kindersley Ltd.; **148BR:** Dorling Kindersley © 2005; **149TL:** Dorling Kindersley © 2005; **149TR:** Dorling Kindersley © 2005; **149C:** Interfoto/History/Alamy; **149BL:** Dorling Kindersley © 2005; **149BR:** Dorling Kindersley © 2005; **150:** Andersphoto/Shutterstock; **150–151Bkgd:** Maksim Kabakou/Shutterstock; **151T:** Yomka/Fotolia; **151B:** Fuse/Getty Images; **152–159Bkgd:** McIek/Shutterstock; **153:** Redmond Durrell/Alamy; **154:** Spiral media/Shutterstock; **155:** Macrovector/Fotolia; **158:** Scratch is a project of the Lifelong Kindergarten group at the MIT Media Lab.; **159T:** Scratch is a project of the Lifelong Kindergarten group at the MIT Media Lab.; **159C:** Scratch is a project of the Lifelong Kindergarten group at the MIT Media Lab.; **159B:** Scratch is a project of the Lifelong Kindergarten group at the MIT Media Lab.; **160–161:** Pamela Moore/E+/Getty Images; **161:** Trantor1911/Fotolia; **162–165Bkgd:** McIek/Shutterstock; **163:** Michael Brown/Fotolia; **166:** Wake Forest Institute for Regenerative Medicine; **167:** Jennifer Owen/Jan Martin Studios; **168:** Amelie-Benoist/BSIP/AGE Fotostock; **169T:** Piero Cruciatti/Alamy; **169B:** Amelie-Benoist/BSIP/AGE Fotostock; **170:** Wake Forest Institute for Regenerative Medicine; **171:** Wake Forest Institute for Regenerative Medicine